THE
CHUNNEL

THE
CHUNNEL

TITLES IN THE BUILDING HISTORY SERIES INCLUDE:

Alcatraz
The Atom Bomb
The Canals of Venice
The Eiffel Tower
The Empire State Building
The Golden Gate Bridge
The Great Wall of China
The Holy City of Jerusalem
The Hoover Dam
The International Space Station
Machu Picchu
The Medieval Castle
The Medieval Cathedral
Mount Rushmore
The National Mall
The New York Subway System
A Nuclear Power Plant
The Palace of Versailles
The Panama Canal
The Parthenon of Ancient Greece
The Pyramids of Giza
The Roman Colosseum
Roman Roads and Aqueducts
The Russian Kremlin
Shakespeare's Globe
The Sistine Chapel
The Space Shuttle
The Statue of Liberty
Stonehenge
The Suez Canal
The Taj Mahal
The Titanic
The Tower of Pisa
The Transcontinental Railroad
The Vatican
The Viking Longship
The White House
The World Trade Center

BUILDING
HISTORY
SERIES

THE
CHUNNEL

by Marcia Amidon Lüsted

LUCENT BOOKS

An imprint of Thomson Gale, a part of The Thomson Corporation

THOMSON

GALE

Detroit • New York • San Francisco • San Diego • New Haven, Conn.
Waterville, Maine • London • Munich

THOMSON
—★—™
GALE

For more information, contact
Lucent Books
27500 Drake Rd.
Farmington Hills, MI 48331-3535
Or you can visit our Internet site at http://www.gale.com

LIBRARY OF CONGRESS CATALOGING-IN-PUBLICATION DATA

Lüsted, Marcia Amidon.
    The Chunnel / By Marcia Amidon Lüsted.
      p. cm. — (Building history series)
Includes bibliographical references and index.
ISBN 1-59018-545-5 (hardcover : alk. paper)
1. Channel Tunnel (England and France)—Juvenile literature. I. Title. II. Series.
TF238.C4L87 2005
624.1'94'0916336—dc22

                                                                  2004022413

Printed in the United States of America

Contents

FOREWORD

Throughout history, as civilizations have evolved and prospered, each has produced unique buildings and architectural styles. Combining the need for both utility and artistic expression, a society's buildings, particularly its large-scale public structures, often reflect the individual character traits that distinguish it from other societies. In a very real sense, then, buildings express a society's values and unique characteristics in tangible form. As scholar Anita Abramovitz comments in her book *People and Spaces*, "Our ways of living and thinking—our habits, needs, fear of enemies, aspirations, materialistic concerns, and religious beliefs—have influenced the kinds of spaces that we build and that later surround and include us."

That specific types and styles of structures constitute an outward expression of the spirit of an individual people or era can be seen in the diverse ways that various societies have built palaces, fortresses, tombs, churches, government buildings, sports arenas, public works, and other such monuments. The ancient Greeks, for instance, were a supremely rational people who originated Western philosophy and science, including the atomic theory and the realization that the Earth is a sphere. Their public buildings, epitomized by Athens's magnificent Parthenon temple, were equally rational, emphasizing order, harmony, reason, and above all, restraint.

By contrast, the Romans, who conquered and absorbed the Greek lands, were a highly practical people preoccupied with acquiring and wielding power over others. The Romans greatly admired and readily copied elements of Greek architecture, but modified and adapted them to their own needs. "Roman genius was called into action by the enormous practical needs of a world empire," wrote historian Edith Hamilton. "Rome met them magnificently. Buildings tremendous, indomitable, amphitheaters where eighty thousand could watch a spectacle, baths where three thousand could bathe at the same time."

In medieval Europe, God heavily influenced and motivated the people, and religion permeated all aspects of society, molding people's worldviews and guiding their everyday actions. That spiritual mind-set is reflected in the most important medieval structure—the Gothic cathedral—which, in a sense, was a model of heavenly cities. As scholar Anne Fremantle so elegantly phrases it, the cathedrals were "harmonious elevations of stone and glass reaching up to heaven to seek and receive the light [of God]."

Our more secular modern age, in contrast, is driven by the realities of a global economy, advanced technology, and mass communications. Responding to the needs of international trade and the growth of cities housing millions of people, today's builders construct engineering marvels, among them towering skyscrapers of steel and glass, mammoth marine canals, and huge and elaborate rapid transit systems, all of which would have left their ancestors, even the Romans, awestruck.

In examining some of humanity's greatest edifices, Lucent Books' Building History series recognizes this close relationship between a society's historical character and its buildings. Each volume in the series begins with a historical sketch of the people who erected the edifice, exploring their major achievements as well as the beliefs, customs, and societal needs that dictated the variety, functions, and styles of their buildings. A detailed explanation of how the selected structure was conceived, designed, and built, to the extent that this information is known, makes up the majority of the volume.

Each volume in the Lucent Building History series also includes several special features that are useful tools for additional research. A chronology of important dates gives students an overview, at a glance, of the evolution and use of the structure described. Sidebars create a broader context by adding further details on some of the architects, engineers, and construction tools, materials, and methods that made each structure a reality, as well as the social, political, and/or religious leaders and movements that inspired its creation. Useful maps help the reader locate the nations, cities, streets, and individual structures mentioned in the text; and numerous diagrams and pictures illustrate tools and devices that bring to life various stages of construction. Finally, each volume contains two bibliographies, one for student research, the other listing works the author consulted in compiling the book.

Taken as a whole, these volumes, covering diverse ancient and modern structures, constitute not only a valuable research tool, but also a tribute to the human spirit, a fascinating exploration of the dreams, skills, ingenuity, and dogged determination of the great peoples who shaped history.

IMPORTANT DATES IN THE CONSTRUCTION OF THE CHUNNEL

1802
French mining expert Albert Mathieu Favier first suggests a Channel tunnel.

1856
Aimé Thomé de Gamond proposes a double tunnel, one of his many plans for a Channel link.

1973
Britain and France agree to a tunnel project; Britain pulls out in 1975 due to financial problems.

1984
British prime minister Thatcher and French president Mitterrand announce their interest in a tunnel between their two countries.

1987
Work begins on the Channel Tunnel.

| 1800 | 1900 | 1975 | 1980 | 1985 | 1990 |

1880
Engineer Sir Edward Watkin begins a tunnel toward France beneath the Channel but stops due to the public's fears of invasion.

1985
The Channel link competition is announced.

1986
Eurotunnel's plan for the Chunnel wins the competition.

1988
The British tunnel boring machine encounters difficult, watery conditions.

1990
The two TBMs meet beneath the Channel, and France and Britain are linked for the first time.

1992
Track installation takes place in the running tunnels.

2001
Hundreds of refugees rush the Chunnel in an attempt to cross into Britain illegally.

1994
The Chunnel is officially open.

| 1990 | 1995 | 2000 | 2005 |

1991
Workers finish drilling the north- and south-running tunnels.

1996
A fire occurs in the Chunnel's south tunnel.

2004
The Chunnel celebrates its tenth anniversary; Eurotunnel plans for a future automobile tunnel.

1993
Track signals are installed and locomotives are tested. The first train, with officials and dignitaries onboard, travels through the Chunnel.

INTRODUCTION

LINKING TWO COUNTRIES

On December 1, 1990, two men reached toward each other and shook hands through a hole drilled in the rock 180 feet below the English Channel. One was an English worker named Graham Fagg, and the other was a Frenchman, Philippe Cozette. It was the first time that men from those two countries had shaken hands while, technically, standing in their own countries. The Chunnel, a rail tunnel that runs beneath the English Channel and links England and France, had reached its first construction milestone. It was the most expensive engineering project in history.

The English Channel, whose geographic name is the Strait of Dover, is a body of water that separates England from France. It is approximately 350 miles long, and its width ranges from 150 miles at its widest point to 22 miles at its narrowest point. In French the Channel is called La Manche, or "the sleeve," because of its long, narrow shape that resembles the sleeve of a garment.

The Strait of Dover is one of the youngest bodies of water on the planet, most likely formed a half million years ago when a glacial lake in the North Sea overflowed and broke through a ridge of chalk stone that ran southeast from what is now England. It is possible that this chalk ridge was a land bridge that once connected England to the Netherlands. Geologists think that this breakthrough of water was catastrophic because it left a huge scar over five hundred feet deep in the seabed, similar to the scar left in a riverbed below a waterfall. The breakthrough created the English Channel as it is today, with the famous sea cliffs called the White Cliffs of Dover in England and the slightly lower sea cliffs of Cap Blanc Nez in France. Because they were formed from chalk stone, both sets of cliffs are known for their distinctive white color.

The English Channel separates England from the rest of the world and has protected England from invasion by hostile countries during several European conflicts. Without the Channel, both Napoleon and Hitler would most likely have succeeded in invading and conquering the British people. Even William Shakespeare makes reference in his play *Richard II* to the important role the Channel played in providing protection for England:

> This fortress built by Nature for herself,
> Against infection and the hand of war,
> This happy breed of men, this little world,
> This precious stone set in the silver sea,
> Which serves it in the office of a wall,
> Or as a moat defensive to a house,
> Against the envy of less happier lands . . .[1]

The Cliffs of Dover form an imposing ridge of chalky-white limestone on the English side of the English Channel, a body of water that separates Britain from France.

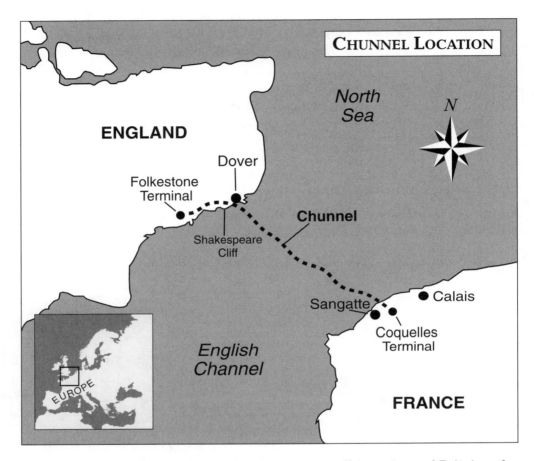

While the Channel did not stop all invasions of Britain—the Romans landed there and occupied Britain around A.D. 43 and William, Duke of Normandy in France, invaded in A.D. 1066—it has been sufficient to repel other major invasions in modern history. Even Adolf Hitler during World War II was not able to invade England via the Channel, even though its English coast was sparsely defended by a Home Guard army with outdated weapons. Because of its isolation Britain has been able to retain a distinct national identity, which it had been extremely reluctant to jeopardize by allowing the construction of a more permanent access between England and France.

With the transportation and commerce needs of the twentieth century, however, it became increasingly apparent that a better method was needed for crossing the English Channel and linking modern Britain to the rest of Europe. Ferries were slow and subject to the weather and harsh conditions of the Channel's currents, often resulting in a miserable crossing for travelers. Even with the advent of air traffic, expense and weather conditions still made this a less than perfect method for crossing the Channel. So with renewed determination, entrepreneurs began to study the Channel with the idea of creating a permanent link between England and France. They eventually decided the Chunnel would be the perfect solution.

A CHANNEL HISTORY

Throughout history the English Channel had been an obstacle to commerce and travel between England and France. From very early on, people tried to devise methods for crossing the Channel by more permanent means such as bridges or tunnels, but because of politics, funding, and the state of technology, none of these schemes ever succeeded. It was not until the twentieth century and a change in the political attitudes of the English and the French that a method for crossing the English Channel with minimal inconvenience was devised, funded, approved, and actually completed.

NAVIGATING THE CHANNEL

The English Channel has always had a reputation for being difficult to navigate by boat and unpleasant for travelers who wish to cross from Europe to England. The tides in the Channel are swift, and there are ridges of sand that rise close to the surface. Dense fog often fills the strait, making it difficult to see. The marine signal station in Dunkirk, France, has determined that there are only sixty days in the entire year when the Channel weather is clear for twenty-four hours, and the chances of experiencing a gale on any particular day are one in seven. Even modern radar and radio often are unable to help ships negotiate the English Channel, making it a dangerous area for shipping. According to Drew Fetherston in his book *The Chunnel: The Amazing Story of the Undersea Crossing of the English Channel:*

> On January 11 [1971], the tanker *Texaco Caribbean* collided with the Peruvian freighter *Paracas*, broke in two, blew up and sank in twenty-three meters [seventy-five feet] of water near the Varne [Varne Bank, a six-mile-long sandbar that divides the English Channel], taking nine of her crew. Before the next dawn, despite heroic efforts by the British lighthouse authority to mark the wreck and warn off other ships, the German freighter

1

Brandenburg struck the tanker wreck and sank, with a loss of seventeen more lives. Although many more lights and buoys were strung about the wrecks, a Greek freighter struck one and sank on February 27. By this time, supertankers were an important part of Channel traffic. They traveled through the Strait, the big passenger ferries traveled across it; it was easy to imagine a nightmare scenario in which one collided with the other.[2]

As many as 600 ships pass through the English Channel every day, at times as many as 120 an hour. In addition to commercial shipping, there are also the ferries that transport passengers from one country to the other. These ferries had a

In 1987 rescue boats come to the aid of a capsized ferry in the English Channel. Throughout history, navigating the channel has been a dangerous task.

reputation for providing a miserable trip across the Channel. Seasickness was frequent, and the trip was usually wet and foggy with very little visibility. Even the great writer Charles Dickens commented on his ferry trip from England to France, "At five in the morning you were blown out of bed, and after a dreary breakfast, with crumpled company, in the midst of confusion, were hustled on board a steam-boat and lay wretched on the deck until you saw France lunging and surging at you with great vehemence over the bowsprit."[3]

EARLY CROSSING PLANS

The miserable conditions that travelers encountered when crossing the Channel by boat gave rise to the earliest plans for a Channel link. As early as 1802 a French engineer, Albert Mathieu Favier, drew plans for a double tunnel that would run beneath the Channel. His plan consisted of building a tunnel for horse-drawn traffic. Running parallel to the tunnel would be a smaller tube for ventilation. A gutter would carry any water that seeped into the tunnels to large pits at each end, where it could be pumped to the surface.

Mathieu, who had worked in coal mines that were considerably deeper than the two-hundred-foot depth of the English Channel, knew that people who were not accustomed to such depths might think that his plan was impossible. However, he made his proposal to Napoleon Bonaparte, the leader of France, who was very interested in improving travel and communication between his country and England. Napoleon mentioned the proposal to the British government during a peace talk as a project that the two countries could undertake together. However, the English government saw things differently. Fearing that Napoleon was more interested in invading England, they would not agree to the plan.

DE GAMOND'S PLAN

The next man to become obsessed with creating a Channel link was a Frenchman named Aimé Thomé de Gamond, who was born in 1807. By the time he was thirty, de Gamond had designed seven different structures to link the two countries, including two tunnels and five bridges. One of his tunnel designs called for an immersed iron tube that would sit on the Channel floor and contain a roadway. A few years later de Gamond had

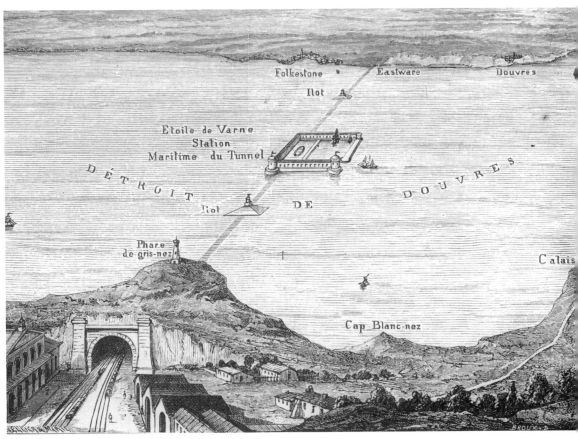

In the mid-nineteenth century, a French engineer by the name of Aimé Thomé de Gamond created this design for a tunnel beneath the English Channel.

even more ideas, such as constructing a huge granite-and-steel bridge with arches high enough for ships to pass beneath.

Most of de Gamond's plans were so far-fetched that they were not taken seriously, although this did not stop him from continuing to create designs for a link. His greatest plan, which he described in a proposal made in 1856, involved tunneling from both sides of the Channel to a point in the middle where an artificial island would be constructed. This island would serve as a port for ships on the surface. A huge spiral ramp would connect the surface of the island to tunnels running underneath the English Channel, which would be lined with brick and would contain two railroad tracks. The tunnel would be ventilated by shafts that would be connected to thirteen more artificial islands spread across the Channel. Each island would have a lighthouse to aid in the navigation of the Channel.

As well as creating elaborate plans for different methods to cross the Channel, de Gamond made other claims about his experiences that tended to make him seem like a dreamer and exaggerator rather than a practical engineer. According to Drew Fetherston in his book *The Chunnel,*

> [de Gamond] tells tales, in his writings, that invite disbelief. For instance, he says that he made several dives in 1855 to the bottom of the Channel to collect rock samples. He made these descents naked except for a cloth band around his head and butter-soaked lint in his ears and nostrils, with a spoonful of olive oil in his mouth to keep water from forcing its way into his lungs . . . with four 25-kilogram bags [over sixty pounds] of stones to carry him down and a string of ten inflated pig bladders to whisk him back to the surface. On one dive . . . he was attacked and bitten on the chin by fish, which later observers think may have been conger eels. Pearl divers make such descents, but whether a forty-eight-year-old civil engineer could survive a plunge to thirty-three meters [108 feet] with such equipment—and whether conger eels would be there to greet him—is a matter of disbelief rather than proof.[4]

Despite his lack of credibility, de Gamond did manage to interest the British queen Victoria as well as several reputable English engineers in his plan for a tunnel and a series of artificial islands. Queen Victoria, who was known to suffer terribly from seasickness, responded to de Gamond's plan by saying, "You may tell the French engineer that if he can accomplish it, I will give him my blessing in my own name and in the name of all the ladies of England."[5]

The plan seemed close to becoming a reality when the Franco-Prussian War erupted, a war declared by France's emperor Napoleon III on Prussia (Germany) in July 1870 in an attempt to gain territory. As a result, the fear that the French might attempt to invade England through the easy access of a tunnel resurfaced and made the tunnel link idea unpopular. De Gamond died penniless in 1876, having spent 175,000 francs (approximately thirty-four thousand dollars) of his own money pursuing his plan.

MORE TUNNEL PLANS

Other people followed de Gamond in the quest to create a Channel link. And Sir Edward Watkin, chairman of two of Britain's railways, actually started an underwater railroad tunnel beneath the Channel. He had the money and the cooperation of a French group to help him, the Société du Chemin de Fer Sous-Marin entre la France et l'Angleterre (Society for an Undersea Railroad between France and England), which had been organized in 1875. This French society was well ahead of the British in planning a tunnel and had already taken thousands of depth soundings and seabed samples along the proposed tunnel route.

In 1879 French workers operate a tunnel boring machine in Sangatte, a port city that eventually became the entrance point for the modern Chunnel.

By 1879 it was already working on the construction of a tunnel access shaft at Sangatte, a city on the French coast that would one day become the entrance point for the modern Chunnel. For the digging of the tunnel, Watkin chose to use a new tunnel boring machine designed by Colonel Frederick Beaumont, which was the prototype for many of the tunnel boring machines used today. This machine, which ran on compressed air, was equipped with fourteen steel cutters set in two revolving arms at the front of the machine. Each turn of these cutters pared away five-sixteenths of an inch of chalk, which was then carried to the back of the machine by a conveyor belt and disposed of by hand carts on narrow gauge railroad tracks.

In 1880 Watkin began a shaft near Shakespeare Cliff on the British side of the Channel and soon had the tunnel boring machine actually grinding a tunnel toward France. Watkin expected to complete a first pilot tunnel (a small tunnel that would serve as a guide for the later, larger tunnels) within five years. In autumn of 1882 the French began tunneling from their side of the Channel with another tunnel boring machine, digging over three hundred feet in a single six-day week.

Watkin was an expert at public relations and routinely invited politicians, statesmen, and reporters to visit the tunnel as it slowly progressed. According to an article in the *London Times* newspaper in July 1881,

> The visitors were lowered six at a time in an iron "skip" down the shaft into the tunnel. At the bottom of this shaft, 163 feet below the surface of the ground, the mouth of the tunnel was reached, and the visitors took their seats on small tramcars which were drawn by workmen. So evenly has the boring machine done its work that one seemed to be looking along a great tube with a slightly downward set, and as the glowing electric lamps, placed alternately on either side of the way, showed fainter and fainter in the far distance, the tunnel, for anything one could tell from appearances, might have had its outlet in France.[6]

While Watkin continued to make progress on the channel link, once again the tunnel came under fire from those in England who feared that it could be used to invade their country. According to Lieutenant General Sir Garnet Wolseley, a re-

spected veteran of the British army, in a government memo-
randum written in 1882, "A couple of thousand men might
easily come through the tunnel in a train at night, avoiding all
suspicion by being dressed as ordinary passengers, or passing

A TUNNELING HISTORY

The idea of digging a tunnel to connect two locations was
not a new idea. There is a long history of tunneling that
stretches back four thousand years. Many towns in the
Middle East needed to have access to water inside the
defensive walls that surrounded them, and by digging
tunnels to a spring or other water source they could find
a secure way to bring water into the town even when it
was under siege. The ancient Babylonians used tunnels
to irrigate their crops, and the Romans were the first to
use fire for tunnel digging when they tunneled almost
five thousand feet from Pozzuoli to Naples, in Italy. They
would set a hot fire burning near the rock and then throw
cold water over the rock face. The sudden change in
temperature would cause the rock to crack.

Underwater tunneling has not occurred nearly as often. The first underwater tunnel, finished in 2180 B.C.,
was a passage for pedestrians under the Euphrates River
in Babylon. Some historians doubt whether this "first"
tunnel actually existed. No trace of it has ever been
found, although details of its construction are mentioned
in the writings of a Greek historian of Julius Caesar's
time. The second underwater tunnel was not completed
until 1843, and it was a thousand-foot-long tunnel beneath the Thames River in London. No other known tunnels were dug underwater in all the time between the
digging of these two tunnels.

Tunneling methods took a great leap forward as technology expanded the world's means of transportation.
The birth of railroads in the nineteenth century created a
great age of tunneling, as engineers came up with new
methods for tunneling through rock for canal, railroad,
and eventually automobile traffic. The Hudson River railroad tunnels were dug late in the nineteenth century to
bring rail traffic right into New York City from New Jer-
sey, eliminating the need for bridges and ferries.

English workmen operate a steam-powered boring machine in a subterranean tunnel. For reasons of national security, work on the original Channel tunnel was halted in the 1880s.

at express speed through the tunnel with the blinds down, in their uniform and fully armed . . . and then England would be at the mercy of the invader."[7]

Even Queen Victoria withdrew her support for the tunnel plan. Watkin tried to assure the British government that the tunnel could be destroyed if the country felt itself in jeopardy from a French attack. He told the British government's examining committee, "I will give you the choice of blowing up, drowning, scalding, closing up, suffocating and other means of destroying our enemies. . . . You may touch a button . . . and blow the whole thing to pieces."[8] But despite his best efforts to win over the politicians of England, Watkin was finally told not to dig his tunnel beneath British lands. The tunneling machine was stopped in 1882, after having dug over six thousand feet of tunnel, and the French machine halted the next year, after five thousand feet.

In the following years other people proposed similar tunneling plans, but they were all rejected by the British government and the British War Office for defense reasons. And World War II put an end to any plan for a Channel tunnel as the British people defended themselves against invasion by Hitler and his German army.

MODERN TUNNEL PLANS

After the Second World War, the idea of a Channel link was no longer subject to military objections. Most British people knew that an invading force would be able to use airplanes and bombs rather than ground troops and ships, and tunnel access would not add any additional risk of invasion. Furthermore, as the 1950s brought peace the focus shifted to transportation and travel. In fact it was yet another horrible trip across the Channel by ship that brought about the next attempt to build a Channel tunnel.

Sisters and French heiresses Izaline and Henriette Doll were crossing the Channel in 1956 when an unexpected storm transformed the two-and-a-half-hour trip into seven hours. The two sisters had wealthy and well-connected husbands, and after complaining about the trip to them, the two men, Frank Davidson and Count Arnaud de Vitry D'Avaucourt, created the Channel Tunnel Study Group. After studying the Channel, the group devised a plan to build a Channel tunnel. The tunnel would be paid for by the investments of banks and private businesses from all over the world instead of the governments of the two countries, although the cooperation of both countries in the construction process was essential. Unfortunately, the tunnel project was doomed by an argument between France and Britain as to whether Britain would be allowed to join the Common Market, which was an economic association of European countries. France did not want Britain to join, so Britain decided that it would not approve construction of a Channel tunnel unless it could join the Common Market. Yet another tunnel project came to a standstill.

Britain eventually joined the Common Market in 1973, and this opened communication between France and England about creating a link between the two countries via the Channel. Despite considering many designs for bridges, submerged tube tunnels, and combinations of both, the original plan for a bored

CROSSING THE CHANNEL

One of the main reasons for building a Channel link between England and France has always been the infamously bad weather and seasickness involved in crossing the Channel by ferryboat. Charles Dickens complained of the dreadful passage, as did several other lesser-known writers, such as François de la Rochefoucauld, a young French nobleman. He describes his crossing, as quoted in Drew Fetherston's book *The Chunnel:*

> At Calais [France] we had waited two days owing to the unfavorable weather and, when we made a start, we experienced one of the most violent sea-voyages possible. For twelve hours we were exposed to most disagreeable buffetings which made me extremely ill during the whole period. Seasickness has an overwhelming quality; at every moment you think you are going to die and there is nothing that can bring you comfort. . . . One must indeed pay tribute to the sea—happy are they whom she spares.

The English Channel is especially notorious for causing seasickness because the cliffs on either side funnel the wind and intensify it. The waves bounce off the cliffs and crisscross other waves, creating swells and hollows in the water that cause boats to turn in circles. These waves are joined by long-distance waves that enter the Channel from the North Sea and become steeper in the shallow water. Strong tidal currents flowing in the same direction as the wind also produce steeper waves. It is no surprise that even Queen Victoria, who suffered from seasickness in the Channel, advocated a Channel tunnel to help travelers avoid the miserable sea crossing.

railroad tunnel was still considered to be the most economical and safest. The governments chose the tunnel option and commissioned a thorough geological investigation of the Channel bed. More than seventy exploratory boreholes were drilled in the seabed to determine exactly what kind of rock and formations were there. This information was important for determining the best route for the tunnel, since certain types of rock were better for drilling through than others. The type of rock lying in the path of the tunnel would also determine how expensive the drilling process would be.

In 1973 work began on the tunnel itself for the first time since Watkin's tunnel in the 1880s. French workers began excavating a huge access shaft on their side, and the British continued to excavate the tunnel begun by Watkin. With both governments in favor of the project, it seemed as if the Channel Tunnel would finally become a reality.

However, in January 1975, after just a few months of work, an economic roadblock stopped the construction of the tunnel once again. Britain was experiencing a severe economic recession with high unemployment and rising inflation. Two hundred thousand British people had lost their jobs, and even banks were in danger of bankruptcy. The government was forced to scrap many government-funded projects that had been in the works, and the tunnel was one of them. The cost of the proposed tunnel and the high-speed railway that would accompany it were enormous, and Britain could not afford them. Despite France's offer to delay the project by a year, Britain cancelled the project altogether. The French were disappointed with their British partners, and a regional French newspaper, *La Voix du Nord*, was quoted as saying, "Without being too pessimistic, nor giving too much weight to symbols, one can't help but think that the abandonment of the tunnel is a bad sign. Is the future equally precarious for the economic and political links that bind the United Kingdom to its partners in the Common Market?"[9]

Another French newspaper, *Le Parisien Libéré*, simply stated, "Great Britain wishes to remain an island."[10]

THE IDEA THAT WOULD NOT DIE

The idea of building a Channel tunnel, however, simply refused to die. During the 1980s different groups began to study the possibilities again. Large construction companies were looking for projects and a project as big as a Channel tunnel would bring many jobs to the French and English regions where the portals of the tunnels would be built. The British economy, however, still did not have the funds for such a massive project. A different kind of funding would be necessary if the project were to take place.

Finally, in November 1984 during an annual Anglo-French summit meeting between French president François Mitterrand

NOTABLE CHANNEL CROSSINGS

The English Channel has always attracted adventurers and sportsmen who wished to make it into the record books by crossing the Channel first or in unusual ways. In 1785 a Frenchman and an American were the first to cross in a gas-filled balloon. The first person to swim across the Channel was Matthew Webb in 1875, and the first woman was Gertrude Ederle in 1926, who beat the record set by male swimmers by two hours. The first airplane crossed the Channel in 1909, and in 1979 a seventy-five-pound aircraft powered by human pedal-power flew over the Channel. The pilot, Bryan Allen, had to pedal continuously for three hours in order to make it across the water. And in 2003 an Austrian skydiver named Felix Baumgartner jumped out of an airplane thirty thousand feet above Dover, England. Wearing a pair of high-tech carbon wings, he free-fell over the Channel and then opened his parachute above Calais, France.

In 1875 Matthew Webb became the first person to swim across the English Channel.

and British prime minister Margaret Thatcher, a decision was made. In a joint statement the two leaders said that "A fixed cross-Channel link would be in the mutual interests of both countries."[11] But even though they were committing themselves to the construction of a link, there was one important stipulation: The link across the Channel could not be built using government money. Anyone interested in building a link would have to find their own funding from investors and other sources. This would protect the government from losing money on the project, and yet the creation of many new jobs could benefit both countries by lessening the widespread unemployment both nations were experiencing.

The two governments appointed a committee made up of both French and British members to study the project and decide how to proceed. It seemed like just another attempt at building the elusive Channel tunnel, but it would prove to be the attempt that finally succeeded.

A WINNING DESIGN

England and France had finally agreed to build a Channel link together, but that announcement was only the beginning of a very long process. There would be many obstacles and struggles to overcome before a link could be built. The problem of financing such an enormous project had to be solved, the exact design for the link had to be decided upon, and a contractor capable of constructing it had to be found.

A CONTEST
On April 2, 1985, the British and French governments made a surprise announcement concerning the Channel link. They issued a formal, sixty-four-page document called "Invitation to Promoters." It was an invitation to anyone who might be interested in building the Channel link to submit a design proposal. Essentially it was a contest to see who could design the best link. In his 1995 lecture "The Making of the Channel Tunnel: A Modern Day Wonder," John Neerhout Jr. describes some of the rules for the contest:

> The closing date for submissions was midnight on October 31, 1985. Attached to each invitation were more than 60 pages of guidelines setting out the competition rules. Each proposer's financial plans were to be presented, including amounts of cash to be raised and money already promised. The link would be constructed and operated at the risk of the chosen promoter, which would be free to decide its own commercial policy, tariffs, and the type of service to be offered.[12]

There were several other stipulations regarding the design: The link had to last at least 120 years, it had to be resistant to terrorist attacks, it had to be very safe for humans, and it could not allow rabid animals to pass from France into England. England had eradicated rabies, an infectious disease found in dogs, cats, and other small animals that can be transmitted to humans through the bite of an infected animal. As an isolated island, it was extremely important to the British that one single rabid animal not cross the Channel from France to Britain undetected. The British feared that a reintroduced strain of rabies could endanger both farm livestock and wild animals as well as humans.

The company interested in building a link also had to prove that it was financially sound and could raise large amounts of money necessary to pay for the project. It also had to be experienced

A DRIVE-THROUGH CHUNNEL?

When plans were being made for a modern Channel link, engineers often attempted to create tunnels that would allow travelers to drive their own automobiles through at least part of the distance. One of the reasons why the Chunnel was built for rail traffic rather than cars is the effects that driving through such a long tunnel can have on a driver. According to Drew Fetherston in his book *The Chunnel:*

> One of the reasons why this tunnel was being built for locomotives rather than automobiles [was that the fluorescent tunnel lights], the visual equivalent of white noise, had a tendency to overpower drivers, to alter the state of their attention to the road. In long road tunnels, some drivers are afflicted with the sensation that their vehicles are creeping sideways toward the wall or toward the oncoming traffic. Eventually, these drivers become paralyzed by fear and simply stop. In the Alps, long road tunnels kept motorcycle outriders on hand to scoot out and rescue these sufferers. Sometimes they had to peel a driver's rigid fingers off the wheel.

With the Eurotunnel Group's plans to add an automotive tunnel across the Channel by the year 2020, making it possible for drivers to enter the tunnel on a highway and drive themselves through, engineers will have to address the problem of lighting and its effects on drivers to make sure that the tunnel would remain as safe as possible.

enough in construction to build the link within a reasonable amount of time. A company entering a design in the contest was required to pay a deposit of approximately $348,000, which would be refunded if its project was rejected. With the deadline for submitting proposals for the project less than seven months away, the contractors had very little time to develop their proposals thoroughly.

The governments promised that they would make a decision by January 1986, when they would either choose one of the proposals or reject them all. It was up to the proposers to utilize the most modern methods available to design a successful Channel link. According to Prime Minister Margaret Thatcher, building a permanent Channel crossing was "a project that can show visibly how the technology of this age has moved to link the Continent and Britain closer together."[13]

BRUBBLES AND BRUNNELS

Once the governments announced the contest, big construction groups from all over Britain and France began to formulate their plans for the perfect Channel link design.

Despite the tremendous costs involved in even planning and submitting a proposal, ten proposals for a Channel link were entered in the contest. The designs generally involved a tunnel, a bridge, or a combination of the two. Tunnels were usually planned to carry rail traffic, since a thirty-mile-long tunnel would not be practical for car traffic. In a tunnel that long, poisonous carbon monoxide from car exhaust would build up in the tunnel. Engineers also worried about the dangers of driving through such a long enclosed tunnel, since the repeating flicker of the tunnel's lighting might mesmerize drivers and make them sleepy. Because of these concerns many of the designs also included a bridge that would still allow people to drive their own cars across the Channel.

Some of the proposals were so complex or fantastic that they could not even be seriously considered. There were plans for building a huge dam similar to the United States' Hoover Dam, with a road on top for cars and a canal lock in the middle for ships to pass through. Another company suggested a bridge with sections that would be supported by gas-filled balloons, eliminating the need for piers or supports in the water. Another proposal called for a suspension bridge whose deck spans

Among the many proposals for a Channel link was a structure similar to America's Hoover Dam (pictured) with a roadway on top allowing cars to cross between England and France.

would be hung from Kevlar fibers. These fibers had never been tested in a bridge construction application, and the plan was quickly eliminated. Another plan included a bridge whose supports would be equipped with hydroelectric generators. These would produce electrical energy from the Channel's tides, which could be sold to help pay the cost of the project.

Another group, headed by an American ferry owner named James Sherwood, proposed a design that called for two huge tunnels bored beneath the Channel. Called the Channel Expressway, these two tunnels would be used by car and truck traffic, but once every hour the automotive traffic would be halted and a train would run through those same tunnels along tracks imbedded in the road. The train's speed would be controlled by a scout vehicle that would go first to make sure that no stray cars were still in the tunnel. The movement of the train would help ventilate the tunnel with fresh air, along with two ventilation shafts and electrostatic scrubbers (machines that collect and remove particles of pollutants from the air) that would help clean the air. This plan would be rejected mostly because the diameters of the tunnels were too large for the geologic conditions beneath the bed of the Channel.

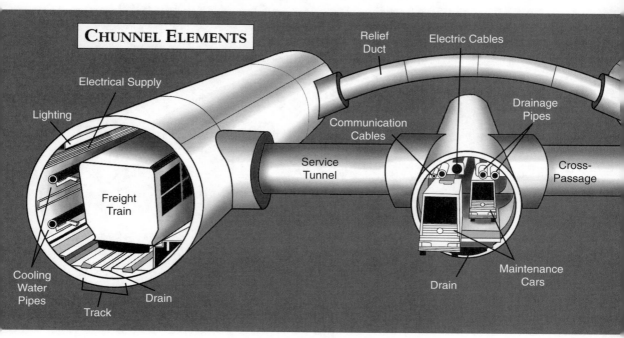

CHUNNEL ELEMENTS

Electrical Supply

Lighting

Freight Train

Cooling Water Pipes

Track

Drain

Relief Duct

Electric Cables

Communication Cables

Drainage Pipes

Service Tunnel

Cross-Passage

Drain

Maintenance Cars

A plan called the Brubble used both a bridge and a tunnel. The bridge would be composed of a big plastic tube containing several decks for cars to drive across, suspended from eight towers built across the Channel. The plastic of the tube would protect the drivers from the Channel's notoriously bad weather. This was one of the most expensive proposals, expected to cost $7 billion. Critics also worried that large ships traveling through the Channel would hit the bridge.

Another plan, the Brunnel, was one of the most popular proposals. It, too, was a bridge and tunnel combination. Travelers would drive their cars out on a bridge that would extend five miles out into the Channel, where there would be an artificial island. At this island, cars would go down a spiral ramp into a thirteen-mile tunnel that would run beneath the Channel. Cars would spiral out of this tunnel again at another artificial island, and then drive along another bridge to the mainland. This plan was somewhat similar to the plan proposed by de Gamond in 1856. Trains would run through a separate tunnel that went the entire twenty-three miles beneath the Channel. This plan was popular because people could drive their own cars across the Channel, but the price was as high as that of the Brubble.

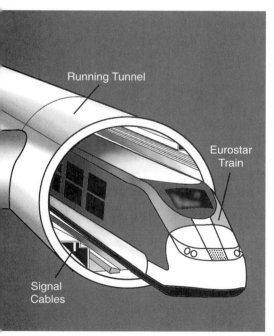

Running Tunnel

Eurostar Train

Signal Cables

The only other plan realistic enough to be seriously considered was a plan called the Chunnel. It was proposed by the Balfour Beatty Construction Company, a large British company that had experience in building huge structures all over the world. The Chunnel design consisted of two parallel railroad tunnels with a smaller service tunnel between them. This plan was not very different from two much earlier plans, the one proposed to Napoleon in 1802 and the tunnel that was started and abandoned in the 1970s. Inside the Chunnel, electric high-speed trains would carry cars and trucks between England and France in just under a half hour. The designers claimed that, with trains leaving every five minutes, they could transport more than four thousand vehicles an hour. This plan would not give passengers the freedom to drive their own vehicles, but its cost, about $3.6 billion, was considerably less than the Brubble and the Brunnel.

A CHOICE IS MADE

A study group of government advisers, engineers, and bankers, with members appointed by both the British and French governments, evaluated all the proposals by December 1985. Before they even began their evaluation, it was assumed by many of the proposing groups that a link allowing for car traffic would be chosen, because of the influence of Margaret Thatcher, the British prime minister. According to Drew Fetherston in his book *The Chunnel* Thatcher was known to hate trains: "One of Thatcher's deepest prejudices [was that] she loathed trains. British Rail embodied everything [she] detested: It was an inefficient, expensive, profitless socialist failure, ruined by bureaucrats and ruled by labor unions. She strongly preferred a link through or over which people might drive themselves."[14] Because of Thatcher's preference for automobiles, many people assumed that a design for a bridge or bridge/tunnel combination for cars would win the competition.

On January 20, 1986, the various companies who had submitted designs for a Channel link gathered in Lille, France, for the official announcement of the winning design. The city was decorated with British and French flags, bands played the national anthems of the two countries, and schoolchildren waved tiny flags. As everyone crowded into a single room, Prime Minister Thatcher said the plan for a link was "a dramatic step in Anglo-French cooperation." French president François Mitterrand called the link "the biggest construction project of the century, representing a grandiose view of the future."[15]

Then the announcement was made: The winning design for a Channel link was the Chunnel, the design submitted by Balfour Beatty. Eventually this company combined with other companies in England and France to form the Channel Tunnel Group/France Manche, which would design, build, and pay for the Chunnel. Their name would be shortened to Eurotunnel.

British prime minister Margaret Thatcher (left) and French president François Mitterrand worked together to choose the winning design for a Channel link.

The Eurotunnel Group actually split into two components to accomplish this huge project. Eurotunnel itself became the group that would operate the tunnel once it was completed. Another division of the company, called the Transmanche Link (TML), would be responsible for the digging and construction work on the Chunnel.

FINDING WORKERS AND MONEY

The biggest issues facing the Eurotunnel project were finding enough experienced people to build such a complex project and finding the money to pay for it. Qualified engineers were difficult to find. A tunnel as large as the Chunnel had never been built before, and the Eurotunnel Group needed the best tunneling engineers available. Unfortunately, it was estimated the project would take seven years or more to complete, and tunneling engineers were used to spending only two or three years on a single project. Most of them were not very enthusiastic about committing to a project for such a long period of time.

One such engineer was a man named Gordon Crighton, who worked for the Balfour Beatty Company and had come

FINANCING THE CHUNNEL

Finding the money for a project as large as the Chunnel involved much more than just approaching one bank and asking for a loan. No single bank could possibly supply the necessary amount of money, a proposed $3.6 billion. Instead, a banking syndicate was formed with three layers of banks involved: the arranging banks, who would gather other banks together to supply the funding; the intermediate banks, who acted as intermediaries between the arranging banks and the lowest tier of banks; and the underwriting banks, who supplied money but had little to do with the actual construction of the Chunnel.

Chris Deacon, who worked for one of the arranging banks, describes the arrangement of banks in Drew Fetherston's book *The Chunnel:* "It was put together on the basis that you'd have about eighty top-quality banks in the deal, banks who understood project financing and were sizeable in terms of capital. We ended up with more than two hundred and twenty banks, with some that never should have been in the deal—some of whom we'd never heard of."

The banks involved in the Chunnel project were from all over the world, including Britain, France, the United States, Japan, and Switzerland. It was only by involving so many different banks that the Chunnel could be built, both in terms of the enormous cost of the project and in spreading the risk. If for some reason the Chunnel did not reach completion and never began to make money from its passengers, then no one lender would have to absorb its enormous debt.

back to England for a few months to help draw up the Chunnel proposal before returning to building a subway in China. When the Eurotunnel Group won the submission contest, he was called back to England again and told that he would be working on the Chunnel project. As quoted in Drew Fetherston's book *The Chunnel*, Crighton was not happy about the assignment:

> I said, "I am not bloody going to take something that is going to last seven or eight years. I am not going." In the construction world, projects last two or three years. Three is a very long project. You get used to moving on to something new every two years. You get bored with it. And I couldn't see myself digging a hole under the Channel, a long boring hole. And so I said no.[16]

Using a combination of pay incentives and persuasion, the company eventually convinced Crighton to accept the job of British tunnel engineering director. He was a valuable addition to the project not only because of his engineering expertise, but because he was Scottish by birth. This gave him an alliance with the British because Scotland was a part of the United Kingdom, and it also worked well with the French because Scotland and France had a past history of uniting together against the British. This made it easier for him to work with both countries' sides of the project.

Eventually the Chunnel project found its workers, both experienced engineers and tunnelers as well as local men who could be taught how to tunnel or do other, less skilled jobs. Approximately 120 skilled workers were hired in six weeks, most of them experienced workers drawn to the project because of its size and importance. Unskilled workers mostly came from the local area, which was experiencing a slow economy and unemployment. Eventually over thirteen thousand people would be employed for the Chunnel project.

Figuring out the financing was also as difficult to settle as finding engineers and workers. With a price tag of $3.6 billion, Eurotunnel needed to find many investors and banks willing to finance the project until it was completed and could begin generating revenue from the price of passage. Eurotunnel sold stock at six dollars a share, meaning that individuals could buy a share of stock and then receive money back once the Chunnel made a profit. Most of the money for the project, however, eventually came from loans from several banks. In total, fifty banks from all over the world, including places such as Japan, Africa, Germany, and Bahrain, contributed money to the Chunnel project in varying amounts.

CHANNEL GEOLOGY

While the issues of engineers and money were being worked out, the Eurotunnel Group also had to refine its design for the Chunnel and submit a more detailed plan. However, before a final design could be drawn up for the Chunnel, the geology of the Channel's bed needed to be studied in more detail. The arrangement and composition of the rock underlying the Channel would affect the success and efficiency of the tunneling process.

The rock that lies beneath the Channel consists of a thick bed of chalk. Chalk is a rock composed of a very pure form of limestone, created millions of years ago when the algae that lived in the warm waters of the ocean died and deposited their skeletons on the sea bed. These skeletons, made of calcite, accumulated slowly over a very long time to form chalk.

The chalk beneath the Channel is composed of three layers, called the Upper, Middle, and Lower Chalk by geologists. The Upper and Middle Chalks are more porous, letting water flow through them, and because of the movement of the earth beneath them, they have been forced near the surface where the turbulent waters of the Channel have cracked and damaged them. Because water passes through them so easily, these layers are not suitable for tunneling. The Lower Chalk layer, however, is different because it has a higher clay content and seals itself against water. The Lower Chalk layer is over 260 feet thick, although it thins to 210 feet near the French coast and extends farther down under the sea. The bottom of this Lower Chalk layer is a substance known as chalk marl, which is even more water-resistant because it contains more clay. Chalk marl has the perfect qualities for tunnelers: It is soft enough to cut through easily, but strong enough to stand up without adding support, although the Chunnel would be lined with concrete for additional strength.

The Eurotunnel builders needed to place as much of the tunnel within the chalk marl layer as possible, even near the French shore where the layer became thinner. It would take

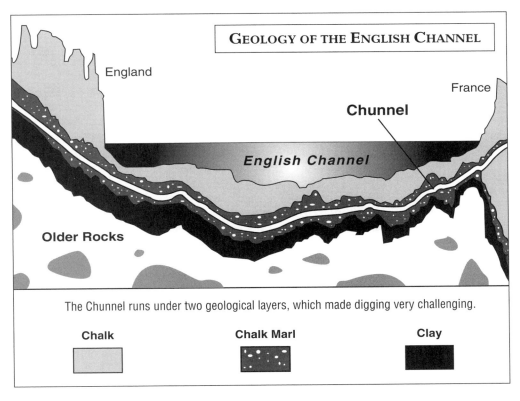

GEOLOGY OF THE ENGLISH CHANNEL

England

France

Chunnel

English Channel

Older Rocks

The Chunnel runs under two geological layers, which made digging very challenging.

Chalk

Chalk Marl

Clay

precise surveying and careful monitoring to keep the tunnel within this layer all the way across the Channel.

THE OFFICIAL TREATY

While these technical preparations were being made for the Chunnel, the governments of Britain and France were also finalizing the political aspects of the construction.

On February 12, 1986, representatives of France and of the queen of England met in Canterbury Cathedral in England to sign the official treaty called Concerning the Construction and Operation By Private Concessionaires of a Channel Fixed Link. This treaty made two groups responsible for overseeing the Chunnel construction: the Intergovernmental Commission and the Safety Authority. These groups were made up of members from both countries. They were to monitor all aspects of the construction and operation of the Chunnel, with the Safety Authority focusing on safety and compliance with the laws of both nations.

THE CONSTRUCTION COMPANIES

The construction of the Chunnel was such a tremendous project that it could not possibly be accomplished by a single construction company. The original Channel Tunnel Group, which submitted the proposal for the Chunnel, was made up of several English and French construction firms: Costain Civil Engineering, Balfour Beatty Company, Taylor Woodrow Construction, and the construction firms of Tarmac and George Wimpey. The French companies included Spie Batignolles, Dumez S.A., Bouygues S.A., SGE, and SAE. The French companies formed a group called Transmanche, and the British companies formed a group called Translink. Together, all the contracting groups formed one group called Transmanche Link, or TML. TML was the construction arm of the Channel Tunnel Group/France Manche, which was later shortened to Eurotunnel. Eurotunnel itself owned and was responsible for running the completed Chunnel. This kept the two arms of the Chunnel project, the builders and the financiers/owners, separate, because many investment banks were unwilling to loan money to an organization that both built and owned the tunnel.

Unfortunately, old concerns about linking England and France permanently with a tunnel were still evident. Several people gathered to protest the project. According to Drew Fetherston in his book *The Chunnel*, "As Mitterrand and Thatcher watched their foreign secretaries sign the treaty, protestors stood behind police lines in the cathedral grounds and shouted their disapproval. Their nationality and the source of their feelings could be deduced from their chant: 'Froggy, froggy, froggy [a derogatory term for French people]—out, out, out.'"[17]

With the signing of the treaty, however, the construction of the Chunnel was set into motion. After more than a hundred years of false starts, it seemed that a Channel link would finally become a reality.

PREPARING TO TUNNEL

Starting the Chunnel was not as easy as simply starting to dig a hole. Before actual digging could take place, the Chunnel's planners had to do the preliminary work, including finding the proper tunnel entrance locations and readying them for construction, digging entrance shafts, and choosing the necessary machinery for the project. A tunnel under such a large body of water could not be dug using old methods of tunneling, either by hand or with existing machines. A new type of tunnel boring machine would have to be used.

TUNNEL BORING MACHINES

The company chosen to supply the special tunnel boring machines needed for the Chunnel project was the James S. Robbins and Associates Company of Seattle, Washington. In 1954 they had invented a successful tunnel boring machine, or TBM, used to dig the water diversion tunnels at the Oahe Dam in South Dakota. These diversion tunnels were vital for redirecting water around the dam site while it was under construction.

The TBMs designed for the Chunnel would be more sophisticated than those first used in the 1950s and would be almost completely automated. Each TBM would be 750 feet long and weigh over fifteen thousand tons. The TBMs would each have a huge rotary cutting head, fifty feet in diameter, with hundreds of cutting edges made of tungsten carbide, one of the strongest materials known to humans. The cutting head would include a rotating disc at the front of a long superstructure of machinery that would include controls to move the TBM, erector arms to line the tunnel, and conveyor belts to carry waste rock away from the cutting surface and bring in the tunnel lining segments. These conveyor belts would terminate at a service train, which would run on tracks like a regular train and would carry the waste out of the tunnel and bring fresh liner segments and supplies in. Author David Macaulay describes the huge cutting heads in his book *Building Big*:

Workers assemble a boring machine for use on the Chunnel. To dig the monstrous tunnel, planners designed elaborate boring machines.

Each [cutting] head [would be] studded with chisel-shaped cutting teeth or inset with steel disks or [have] a combination of the two. As it slowly rotated, the cutting head [would carve] a series of concentric rings of hills and valleys in the chalk marl. The natural stresses in the rock [would cause] the hills to split off as the valleys between them reached a certain depth. The pieces of stone [would fall] through spaces in the cutting head and onto the first part of the conveyor system that [would carry] it all back to waiting spoil cars at the rear of the service train.[18]

A ring of hydraulic rams, which are fluid-powered arms that exert tremendous pushing force, would steer and push the cutting head against the rock surface, forcing it to cut the rock. Another set of rams would force large gripper pads against the walls of the tunnel to provide a firm surface for the steering and thrusting rams to push against. These areas were to be enclosed by protective metal shielding that would keep rock and debris from falling into the machinery. Behind these gripper pads was the control room, where the TBM driver would sit and monitor the machine's movement, although he would have no view of the actual rock cutting at the front of the machine. The TBM could tunnel at a rate of about fifteen feet per hour.

Behind the TBM's control room was an erector arm, which would install segments of the tunnel lining. These segments were concrete rings that would support the newly dug tunnel and prevent it from caving in. Eight hundred feet behind the TBM was the service train, which would deliver the lining segments as well as clean air, compressed air, water, and electrical power. The waste rock from the cutting head, which is called spoil, was to be carried away on a conveyor belt inside the body of the machine, and another conveyor belt would bring the lining segments to the erector arm. The spoil would be dumped into railroad wagons, which would take it to the surface for disposal.

The TBMs were so large that they had to be transported to the work site in pieces and then assembled underground within the tunnel itself. They were also built to dig just one size diameter of tunnel and so they would usually only be used for the one project and then be scrapped.

The Chunnel TBMs were also designed for dry tunneling, since the tunnelers fully expected to stay firmly within the water-impervious chalk marl layer beneath the Channel. Unfortunately, the French side of the tunnel would prove to have more water leakage, and the Robbins Company built a special waterproof version of the TBM that was half TBM and half submarine. This machine, which the French affectionately named Brigitte, was able to withstand the enormous weight of the Channel's water bearing down on the French end of the tunnel. In total the

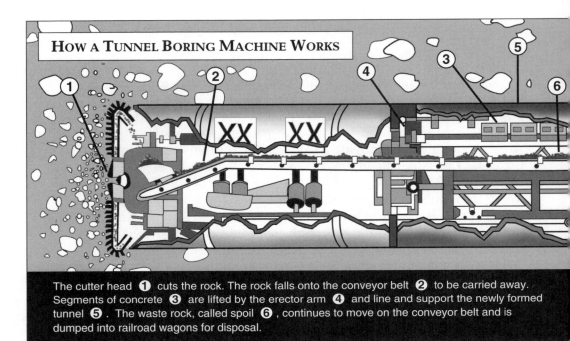

HOW A TUNNEL BORING MACHINE WORKS

The cutter head ❶ cuts the rock. The rock falls onto the conveyor belt ❷ to be carried away. Segments of concrete ❸ are lifted by the erector arm ❹ and line and support the newly formed tunnel ❺. The waste rock, called spoil ❻, continues to move on the conveyor belt and is dumped into railroad wagons for disposal.

Chunnel project required eleven tunnel boring machines at a cost of $90 million.

SHAKESPEARE CLIFF

Once the Chunnel project secured the TBMs, they still needed to find a way to get the machinery into the starting point of the tunnels. This required digging access shafts on both the English and French shores.

There would also need to be sufficient facilities to receive the vast amounts of spoil (the excavated chalk from the tunnels) as it was brought out from the work area. It was estimated that over 141 million cubic feet of spoil would be excavated from the British end of the tunnel alone. It was not efficient, in terms of time or money, to transport this waste rock over a large distance.

On the English side of the Channel, geography did not help the tunnel builders. The English end of the tunnel was located at Shakespeare Cliff, which was on top of the famous White Cliffs of Dover, the white chalk cliffs along the English Channel that were one of England's most beloved landmarks. Shakespeare Cliff was the best starting point because it was there that the Channel was the narrowest. Shakespeare Cliff was five miles from the village of Folkestone, and the closest large city was Dover. Lower Shakespeare Cliff, where the tunnel would actually begin, was just a small ledge stacked with leftover tunnel lining segments from the failed 1974 Channel tunnel project. There was a small access road for vehicles, carved into the cliff between the two areas, but it was so narrow that two vehicles could not pass each other.

The county of Kent, where Shakespeare Cliff was located, did not want the tunnel spoil dumped anywhere on the surrounding

A conveyor removes excavated chalk, or spoil, from the English side of the Chunnel. Establishing facilities where vast amounts of spoil could be disposed was a challenge in itself.

countryside because it would be unsightly and environmentally unfriendly. They were also reluctant to have a concrete factory for the tunnel liner segments built anywhere nearby. The best solution for both of these problems would be to dump the tunnel spoil into the sea at the base of the cliff, enlarging the small land platform that was already there. The resulting land could be used as a marshalling area for tunnel construction, where equipment could be unloaded and stored and a concrete plant could be built. There would also be rail access to the site, since British Rail already had a shore line between

LIFE ON THE SITE

Building the Chunnel required an enormous number of workers. Before World War II many tunnelers working in England came from the roughest part of London. After the war the tunnelers were predominantly Irish. Many of these men had built tunnels all over the world in places such as Hong Kong, Sri Lanka, Egypt, and the United States, and most traveled from job to job. The opportunity to work on a project as big as the Chunnel attracted some tunnelers, but did not appeal to those who were used to working on shorter-term projects.

The tunnelers working on the British end of the Chunnel lived in a special camp built for them by TML. It contained forty-two buildings much like army barracks, each with twenty-eight single rooms. The camp was called Farthingloe Village, and it also had a restaurant, general store, chapel, laundry, barbershop, gymnasium, and two bars. Single workers lived in Farthingloe, while those who traveled with their families lived in a trailer camp nearby.

Working in the tunnel was dangerous and unpleasant: The machinery generated high temperatures and the water used to keep dust down and wash the machines made it extremely humid. The temperature was often 100°F and nearly 100 percent humidity. Workers had to drink gallons of water and work in mud and water for eight hours at a time. In the winter they might rarely see daylight between their shifts underground. It was not an easy job, and yet some workers spent all their working lives on tunneling projects.

Dover and Folkestone, which would ensure the easy delivery of materials.

However, the government of Britain would not allow TML to simply dump tons of soggy chalk spoil into the Channel. They required the builders to enclose the area with a seawall, which would keep the chalk from leaching into the Channel. The seawall would need to be so solidly sealed that none of the chalk could leak through or under the barrier. This would require a huge, sheet metal seawall and would end up as the largest structure ever built from sheet steel pounded into place around concrete. In all, the construction of the seawall required 35,800 tons of steel and over 6 million cubic feet of concrete.

When finished, the resulting area of land would consist of approximately seventy-three acres. The spoil from the tunnel could actually be piled above the level of the seawall, and the highest portion of the site would eventually be over fifty feet above sea level. Once the Chunnel was completed, TML intended to create a nature conservation area on the site, with footpaths and picnic areas. This area would eventually be named Samphire Hoe, and would be managed by the White Cliffs Countryside Project on behalf of Eurotunnel.

OTHER PREPARATIONS

The problem of where to dump the tunnel spoil was solved, but there were other projects that needed to be completed before the actual tunneling could begin. The British tunnelers enlarged an old access shaft from the 1975 tunnel project to use for a marshalling chamber, where TBMs could be assembled. Another tunnel was hand-mined beneath the marshalling site for the conveyor belt that would carry the spoil away from the TBM and out to the surface for disposal. Finally, a 360-foot-deep vertical shaft, which would carry workers and small supplies down to the tunnels in elevators, was dug from the Upper Shakespeare Cliff. Upper Shakespeare Cliff was the site for the offices of the engineers and crew managers and the area where the workers reported for their shifts.

These projects were actually large tasks in themselves, involving large amounts of tunneling and the removal of over 5 million cubic feet of spoil. The passages were created by using both old and new tunneling techniques, including tunneling with hand tools as well as machinery. Rather than lining these passages with concrete or cast-iron rings, they were lined using a new method that involved spraying the excavated surfaces with a special form of concrete called shotcrete.

SANGATTE

While the British were preparing to tunnel on their side of the Channel, the French were also making their own preparations. The French construction site was located in Sangatte, a tiny village on the Channel coast about two miles from the town of Coquelles and four miles from the large city of Calais. The French decided on a different method than the British used for creating access to the tunneling area and a place to assemble their TBMs. Because the ground on the French side was composed of fractured chalk and sand, water had been a constant problem in previous attempts to tunnel directly from the surface as the British had done.

The first task was to dig a huge cylinder-shaped access shaft 230 feet deep and 180 feet in diameter. Surrounding this shaft was an enormous concrete and steel cofferdam 318 feet wide, over 600 feet long, and reaching almost 200 feet down into the ground to the impermeable chalk marl. The cofferdam would keep water from leaking into the access shaft and prevent the walls from caving in. The huge access shaft, nicknamed *le puits de Sangatte* ("the well of Sangatte"), was in itself an engineering wonder.

A platform was constructed 150 feet down in the shaft, with access to six large chambers in the shaft wall, where the TBMs were assembled in dry conditions and the concrete lining segments were brought in. The very bottom of the shaft would be used for bringing out the tunnel spoil. The French had also chosen a different method for disposing of the spoil. They decided to crush it and mix it with water to form slurry, or a watery soup, and then pump it out of the tunnel through a pipeline to a basin a little over a mile away. Six slurry pumps and five huge crushers and mixers sat in the bottom of the Sangatte shaft to handle the spoil. The slurry basin, called the Fond Pignon, was a depression on top of a nearby hill, where the slurry could be dumped and the water would slowly drain away. Eventually a new hill would be formed by the mounds of spoil, and once the project was finished, it would be planted and landscaped.

The Sangatte shaft was the primary work area for the French tunneling teams. Once the shaft was excavated and

WORKING CONTRASTS

The Chunnel was a joint project between two countries, and the way the work was done on either end illustrated the differences in work environments and methods between France and England. These differences also reflected the differences in the cultures of the two countries. The French preferred a clean and organized work environment, whereas the British made do without special frills or luxuries for their workers. On the British side, workers changed their clothes in crowded locker rooms and then went down into the tunnel through a maze of shafts, lugging gas masks in case methane, a toxic gas released from the earth, was present. The French workers had a large room called the *salle des pendus*, or "the hall of the hanged men," because each man had a chain that ran through a pulley in the ceiling. Clothes and belongings were attached to the chain and then pulled up to the ceiling for storage, and the clothes looked very much like hanging bodies. French workers boarded a work train that went down into the shaft on a huge elevator.

There were differences in the workers hired, as well. The British hired experienced tunnelers, who knew how to do the job but were also opinionated as to how it should be done. The French preferred to hire unskilled men and then train them to do the job exactly as they wanted them to. French engineers preferred to have a well-organized plan with clearly defined tasks, whereas the British engineers preferred to plunge into the project and deal with situations as they arose. One of the biggest challenges of building the Chunnel was to get these two different approaches to work together.

A French Chunnel worker enjoys his lunch in the salle des pendus *("hall of the hanged men"), named for the chains that hung from the ceiling.*

French workers built a concrete and steel cofferdam like this one to surround the cylindrical shaft that created construction access to the Chunnel on the French side.

lined with concrete, two huge hangars called naves were built over the shaft to protect it from weather. The shaft had five elevators to bring workers and small equipment down to the platform level: two small elevators and three large enough to transport as many as eighty men—the number of workers that rode a single work train into the tunnel. One of the nave shed roofs was also equipped with a gantry crane that could carry over four hundred tons, enough to lower the pieces of the TBM into the shaft. There were also two sixty-ton cranes for lowering the sections of tunnel lining.

PLANNING THE CHUNNEL'S PATH

While the preliminary work was being done on both shores to get ready for the tunnel excavation, the engineers on the tunnel project were involved in the final design work for the Chunnel. Despite the earlier geological surveys of the Channel's seabed, the engineers quickly discovered that they needed more information in order to determine the best path for the Chunnel.

They needed to drill boreholes into the seabed to extract a core sample that showed the engineers and geologists what types and amounts of certain rocks were located at various depths. Certain types of chalk underlying the Channel were better for tunneling than others, and choosing a path through the best type of chalk would make the digging process easier, less expensive, and safer.

The many boreholes that had been dug in previous tunneling attempts were now a hazard to the engineers planning the Chunnel. Too many boreholes would compromise the safe construction of the Chunnel, and digging new holes in the vicinity of the old ones would make the problem worse. If the tunnel itself crossed the path of one of these old boreholes, it would essentially become a pipe feeding Channel water down into the new tunnel. Complicating the problem was the fact that some of the holes drilled in the 1960s had not even been charted on a map.

Another hazard that the engineers worried about was the possibility of finding old, unexploded bombs that might have been dropped or deposited on the Channel floor by the Germans during World War II. If a bomb had penetrated deep enough to lie in the tunnel's path, it would explode when the TBM encountered it. Fortunately, after consulting with the military the TML group felt that it was highly unlikely that any bombs could have reached that depth.

While the engineers needed the additional geological information they would gather from their own boreholes, the timing was not good for collecting these samples. According to Drew Fetherston in *The Chunnel*, the engineers started their drilling in the fall instead of the calmer summer months:

At first, TML tried drilling in sixty meters [196 feet] of water from a ship, with poor success; the currents in the Channel were too strong and pulled the drill bit out of plumb. The first borehole was so delayed and so expensive that the designers thought it would be impossible to complete the borehole campaign. Each hole would require extra vessels to steady the drill ship, and [they] could only get permits to work in the Channel for short periods of time. If bad weather forced the ships to seek shelter—and it was by this time October, when gales were common—the permits might expire.[19]

The problem was finally solved by renting a fixed oil-drilling platform, complete with crew, which drilled twelve boreholes at a cost of $149,000 each. The cores were drilled to a depth of almost a thousand feet and helped the designers shift the path of the tunnel slightly to keep it in the best digging conditions possible. According to a lecture on "The Making of the Channel Tunnel," given by John Neerhout Jr. in 1995:

> After extensive geological surveying, the route of the three tunnels was drawn to run mainly through a layer of soft impermeable (or waterproof) rock called chalk marl. It would be harder to find a better medium for tunneling purposes. The chalk marl allowed the tunnel boring machines (TBMs) starting from the British coasts to be designed for rapid advance, and these TBMs often completed over 300 meters [over nine hundred feet] of tunnel in a week. Near the French coast, there is a stretch of fissured [cracked] water-bearing [soggy] ground. To overcome this difficulty, slower and more complex TBMs, that could operate in a sealed mode under water pressure, were used.[20]

At the French end of the tunnel the cracks in the rock, which were essentially faults in the rock layers, were unstable and likely to shift and cause problems, especially in the event of an earthquake. The engineers would have to keep a close eye on conditions at that end of the tunnel, both during construction and after the Chunnel was complete, in order to maintain the safest and strongest tunnel structure possible.

STAYING ON TRACK

With the Chunnel's course laid out through the seabed of the Channel, the greatest challenge would be to keep the TBMs moving along that course. Since drilling would begin from both sides of the Channel at the same time, it was absolutely imperative that the two machines were exactly aligned on the same path; otherwise, they might not meet at the same point in the middle. If the alignment of the two tunnels was off by less than eight feet, the TBMs could turn enough to make a slightly kinked passage. But TBMs cannot back up, because the automatic placing of the tunnel lining behind the cutting head makes the tunnel smaller in diameter than the TBM itself. So, if

French and English surveying teams check data to confirm that the two ends of the Chunnel are properly aligned.

the two tunnels were off by more than eight feet, the TBMs would have to be disassembled and readjusted and the tunnel lining segments removed, resulting in a costly delay and bad publicity.

To keep the Chunnel on the proper course, the surveyors and engineers developed a laser-guidance system that relied on the newest technology. Because of the underwater depth of the Chunnel, high-technology satellite mapping such as the Global Positioning System (GPS), which relies on satellite information to produce accurate maps, could not be used. Instead, the engineers used a red laser to send a beam of light forward in the tunnel, aimed at a sensitive target on the back of the TBM's cutting head. The point at which this beam hit the target would tell the computers aboard the service train behind the TBM whether or not the drill was on course and which way it needed to turn. This system was not foolproof, since it still depended on the accuracy of the surveyors who aimed the tunnel laser.

Despite this advanced laser system, the project still required surveyors who used traditional instruments to site a straight course through the tunnel. Eric Radcliffe, the chief surveyor on the Chunnel, had to deal with the tunnelers and the limited space inside the tunnel as he attempted to keep the Chunnel on the right course. He constructed a tall concrete wall or plinth to hold his surveying instruments at the place where the access tunnel curved for the start of the first tunnel. According to Drew Fetherston in *The Chunnel* this caused a problem with the engineers:

> When the tunnelers began laying rail for the work trains, they found the plinth sticking out into their path. The se-

A WOMAN'S WORLD

Tunneling had long been considered a man's occupation, often because women were less likely to want the wandering life of a professional tunneler. When the Chunnel project began there were very few women working in the actual tunneling part of the job. There were not even any women's bathrooms on the Chunnel construction site. One of the women who did work on the Chunnel was Helen Nattrass, a geologist and the senior geotechnical engineer for the tunnel construction. She was described as an unusual woman: She drank beer and followed the horse races like the men, but she also played many musical instruments and spoke seven languages. She was warned, when interviewing for the Chunnel job, that she might have difficulty dealing with the attitudes of all the men around her. Nattrass was successful, however, because she gained a reputation as a tough supervisor and earned the respect of the thirty male geologists who worked with her.

Despite the use of a sophisticated laser-guidance system, traditional surveyors like this man were called upon to help site a perfectly straight course through the tunnel.

nior construction engineer came to Radcliffe and told him it would have to be moved. Radcliffe explained that it was absolutely necessary, that there was no other place for it. The engineer dug in his heels.

"I'm not setting off for France with a kink in my track," he said.

"If you move the plinth, you won't know where France *is*," Radcliffe replied. The plinth and the kink remained.[21]

With the access shafts and marshalling chambers built, and the tunnel's course set, it was time to bring in the TBMs and start on the long dig from England to France.

TUNNELING

With the men and equipment ready, it was time to begin excavating the Chunnel. Everyone involved in the project knew that it would be both exciting and extraordinarily difficult. Digging a tunnel beneath the English Channel involved challenges for the engineers and builders that had never been encountered before in dry land tunneling. It took innovative techniques and machinery to accomplish this task in a timely and economical manner.

A DOZEN TUNNELS

As the engineers prepared to lower the pieces of the TBMs into the marshalling chambers, they were not just preparing to dig one tunnel across the Channel. The Chunnel would actually be a complex of a dozen tunnels in all. On the English side, six tunnels would begin under Shakespeare Cliff, three of which would go under the Channel toward France. The other three would go back in the opposite direction, almost five miles to the Folkestone portal where the terminal would be built and passengers would board the trains for France.

The tunnels would be similar on the French side, with three tunnels heading from Sangatte toward England, and three heading back to Coquelles, the French terminal. David Macaulay describes the layout of the tunnels in his book *Building Big:*

> The Channel Tunnel is really three tunnels that run parallel to one another for most of the [twenty-four-mile-long] journey. The northernmost tunnel carries trains from Britain to France, the southern one from France to Britain, and a smaller service tunnel travels between them. Its primary function is to provide access to the main "running" tunnels for periodic maintenance and to serve as an escape tunnel if some kind of problem arises. . . . All three tunnels are linked by cross-passages approximately every 1200 feet.[22]

58

STARTING THE TBMs

The first tunnel to be constructed was the middle service tunnel. The pieces of the huge TBMs were lowered into the marshalling chambers and assembled. The massive cutting head was lowered first, as it would be the first part of the machine into the tunnel. Next the service train that held the hydraulic engine that powered the TBM was installed. Then the conveyor belts that would carry the waste rock out of the tunnel were connected, one end to the TBM's cutting head and the other end to the service train.

On December 1, 1987, the British TBM began to chew its way through the chalk, starting in the abandoned hole where the 1974 tunnel project had begun. British workers had to cut apart and remove the cutting head from the old TBM used during the 1974 project before the new TBM could head toward

In 1988 an engineer guides the crane lowering into place one of the TBMs that will be used to dig the Chunnel's complex of tunnels.

France. At the same time, the French TBM was heading for Britain. If everything went according to plan, the two machines would meet in exact alignment in the middle of the tunnel.

Each TBM had a small probe, a drill that was attached to the front of the TBM. It drilled a small hole to check on the rock conditions before the TBM started cutting in the chalk layer. The probe told the engineers if the chalk marl rock layer was climbing or diving out of the tunnel's path, since it was essential that the TBM maintain a path through the chalk marl layer.

As the TBMs started digging their way across the Channel, an engineer named David Denman described what it was like to be in the tunnel: "Oh, [the TBM] sounds lovely. Magic. You've got the throb of the hydraulic motors, the crunch and whirring of the cutter. You've got to take the *smell* into it—the smell of the ground, the smell of the hot hydraulic oil. To hear the pumps start up, oh, it's wonderful. You can *sense* when you've got a good shift going. You can *smell* it."[23]

Although the TBMs were slowly moving toward each other, there was more to constructing the Chunnel than just digging the hole and putting a railroad through it. The chalk walls alone would not be able to withstand the pressure of the Channel waters over many years. All of the tunnels needed to be lined with concrete, or sometimes even steel, to keep them as safe and sturdy as possible.

THE CONCRETE LINING

Lining the tunnels required careful engineering. The lining had to be thick enough for safety purposes but not require so much concrete that it would increase the cost of the tunnel. Concrete tunnel lining segments had been used on the earlier Channel tunnel project. During the 1975 attempt to build a Channel tunnel, the engineers working at that time installed strain gauges in the tunnel walls to measure the reaction of concrete tunnel lining segments to the pressure of the earth and water above them. The Chunnel engineers were able to use the information from these gauges to help them determine how thick the concrete segments needed to be to keep the new tunnel safely supported. They found that the tunnel lining could actually be a little thinner than the 1975 segments, partly because of a better understanding of the area's geology and also because of the advances in concrete technology.

TUNNELING RATES

There was an informal competition between the French and British tunneling crews to see who would cover the most distance and "win" the race to cross the border of the other's country. It was not possible to declare a true winner, however, since the British TBM might be told to stop at a certain point and await the French TBM's breakthrough.

Both countries' tunnel boring machinery did produce some impressive statistics regarding how quickly they chewed through the chalk marl beneath the English Channel. On its best day the British TBM advanced 247 feet beneath the Channel, and the French TBM advanced 183 feet. In its best week the British TBM tunneled over 1,400 feet, and the French tunneled 959 feet. All together, the TBMs that dug the Chunnel managed to move through roughly one hundred miles of rock in just four years.

The segments would be constructed out of a special kind of concrete, even stronger than the type of concrete used in nuclear power plants. Not only would the concrete segments need to withstand the pressure of the water pushing down constantly on the tunnel, they would also have to withstand a condition called concrete cancer, which is a deterioration that results from seawater penetrating the concrete and corroding the steel reinforcements.

The special concrete would be made from cement, pulverized fuel ash (also called fly ash, the residue left after burning coal), crushed granite, and a compound called a superplasticizer, which reduces the water in the cement and makes it thicker and easier to use in applications where it is heavily reinforced with steel. Superplasticizers also increase the strength of the concrete itself. The Chunnel segments would then be molded around a welded steel wire cage for additional strength.

MAKING CONCRETE SEGMENTS

Plants for producing these concrete lining segments would be built by both the English and the French, each at their own end of the Chunnel. Although the best spot for the production was

A tunneler pumps grout behind a section of concrete lining. The tunnel lining was made of a special concrete capable of withstanding terrific pressure.

right at the mouth of the tunnel, there was not enough room on the English side for a concrete plant. The British finally found an unused oil refinery site on the Isle of Grain, about three hours by rail from the Folkestone terminal site. Because there was a direct rail link, the segments could travel with a minimal amount of loading and unloading. This was extremely important since the concrete plant would ship 422,755 lining segments to the Chunnel site during its three and half years of operation. These segments required over 220,000 tons of cement, almost 100,000 tons of pulverized fuel ash, and 49,000 tons of reinforcing steel. The enormous amount of granite needed came from a mountain in Scotland.

The Isle of Grain concrete production plant took eleven months to build. It contained eight parallel assembly lines, four concrete mixing plants at the edge of the water, storage areas, huge overhead cranes, and railroad track spurs that ran between the production lines. Making the tunnel segments required a lot of hand assembly: There were thirty-five different types of tunnel lining segments, varying in thickness, shape, and the types of holes molded into them. These holes were used for pumping grout behind the installed segments, as well as for attaching brackets for wires and pipes inside the tunnel. Each segment also had a cast-iron-lined socket that could be used to lift the completed piece.

Drew Fetherston describes the concrete segment assembly line in his book *The Chunnel:*

> Each production line had nine workstations, where the molds were cleaned, prepared, fitted with reinforcing cages and filled with concrete. Each station was supposed to finish its work in ten minutes. Segments then moved to curing tunnels, where they were bathed in steam at 50 degrees C [122 degrees F] for six hours. They were then lifted from the molds, wrapped in special jackets to guard against thermal shock and too-rapid drying, and stockpiled outside. If all went well, a production line could turn out 144 segments a day. At peak, the eight lines could fill three 24-car trains a day with segments.[24]

The segment production plant on the French side of the Chunnel was quite different from the British plant. They were able to construct their plant right next to the Sangatte shaft, so the completed segments were simply moved by crane from production down into the shaft and to the tunnel. The French plant was also smaller, since it would only be producing 252,000 segments, but because of the difficult tunneling conditions they were producing seventy-two different types of segments. The French plant was also more automated, with machines rather than people assembling the steel reinforcing cages and computerized cranes moving the pallets of lining segments.

INSTALLING THE SEGMENTS

Once the completed lining segments had been taken into the tunnel on the work train, they were placed on a conveyor belt on the TBM. Each round segment of tunnel lining was actually made up of nine smaller segments, since a complete ring of concrete would be very difficult to install in the tunnel. The individual segments were carried up to an erector behind the cutting head of the TBM, which held them in place. Eight segments were installed in a ring, with a final, smaller segment called the key rammed into place much like a wedge to complete the ring and keep it in place. The completed tunnel lining segment was a small tube of concrete that completely fit into the newly dug section of tunnel. The service tunnel, being slightly smaller, only required six segments and a key. The French end of the tunnel consisted of five segments and a key. The segments were all bolted to each other and to the next ring. The French also installed gaskets, or layers of flexible watertight material, between each ring to make them more watertight, since their rings were under more pressure from the weight of the Channel water above the cracked rock at that end of the Chunnel's path. Both the British and the French pumped grout, a very thin cement, behind the completed rings to make them even more resistant to water.

Each completed ring of tunnel wall weighed over forty tons, and in all a half million slabs of concrete were used to line the Chunnel. The segments used to line the cross-passages and the piston relief ducts were made of cast iron.

THE CONSTRUCTION RAILWAY

The key to supplying the TBMs with the necessary lining segments, as well as transporting other materials and the workers themselves, was the narrow gauge construction railway. A narrow gauge railway has rails that are closer together than normal railroad tracks and is better suited for small spaces. There were more than 120 miles of track laid in the tunnels, and another 8 on the surface at Lower Shakespeare Cliff. This technically made the construction railway the third largest railway in Britain, and trains used on the construction railway logged enough miles every month to circle the earth four times.

The cars on these trains were specifically arranged to deliver the correct tunnel lining segments in the proper order, since not all lining segments were the same. The trains also carried rails to extend the construction railway, ducting for the ventilation system, grout, concrete, fresh water, and materials for the cross-passages.

Workers rode to and from the tunnel site on special cars called manriders. They were flat cars with benches, and at first they had no doors or sides until exhausted tunnelers, dozing on their way back from their work shift, fell asleep and dangled a foot outside of the car, where they would usually be injured by

A machine bolts a segment of concrete lining into place. For ease of installation, each segment of tunnel lining was actually made of nine smaller segments.

French workers weld rails into place along the construction railway that served to transport workers and materials throughout the tunnel.

other equipment in the very crowded tunnel. After several such incidents, the cars were outfitted with steel pipe railings. A heavy net of steel mesh webbing covered the car to prevent injury from falling debris. Some of the manrider cars were self-propelled and did not require a locomotive.

The entire construction railway was so cramped that only one train could run at a time, using a single track. The movements of all the work train locomotives were controlled by one person called the operations board controller, who communicated with the locomotive drivers by radio. There were 183 locomotives in the construction railway fleet, as well as over a thousand rail cars of different types, from tipping hopper cars to carry spoil, to flat cars and manriders, concrete-mixing cars, and other miscellaneous cars.

TUNNELING MISHAPS

Tunneling continued somewhat smoothly on the Chunnel early in 1988, as Gordon Crighton on the British side and Laurent Leblond (the French tunnel engineering director) on the French side oversaw operations from their respective offices. It was hoped that the two TBMs would meet in the middle of the Channel in approximately a year.

Unfortunately, the French TBM "Brigitte" soon stopped dead in the tunnel. A waterproofing seal designed to protect the TBM from seawater was allowing the salty water to leak onto the machine, eating away at the metal because of the high salt concentration. Eurotunnel executives were afraid that if the project were stopped, it would be difficult to restart it with all of the banks, governments, and contractors involved in the project. Instead engineers developed a new seal for Brigitte. The seal was created out of paper and a special type of grease and was placed over the metal joints in the TBM's exterior. When the paper became wet and expanded, a completely waterproof seal would form to protect the metal. However, by the time the engineers found a solution, the Chunnel project was nine months behind schedule.

Then in late March 1988, the British TBM struck bad ground for tunneling. The presence of some water was never unusual in a tunneling project, and since they were tunneling under a large body of water, the TBMs were equipped to pump large amounts of water in case there was a huge inrush at the front of the tunnel. The pumping system was large enough and fast enough to allow the men to exit the tunnel safely. The water problem that TML usually encountered in the British tunnel was caused by overbreak: water-soaked layers of rock overhead that break apart and fall into the tunnel behind the TBM. This was a hazard to the workers who were assembling the concrete liner rings behind the TBM and were vulnerable to rock falling from above them. The usual method for dealing with overbreak was to use cast-iron tunnel lining segments, which could be bolted together in the safety of the shielding right behind the TBM's cutting head, rather than concrete. The concrete segments could not be preassembled under this shielding, since they had to be put into place one by one and then finished with the key segment. Cast-iron segments, however, were more expensive in terms of both time and money. Although the tunnelers on the British side had expected to find some less than perfect tunneling conditions, they soon encountered an area that was worse than they had planned for. In March 1988 the British TBM ran into almost four miles of bad ground. Stephen Johnson and Roberto T. Leon in their book *Encyclopedia of Bridges and Tunnels* describe the situation:

> The French, anticipating wet, porous ground, constructed waterproof boring machines while the British, armed with incorrect geological data, employed ma-

WATER PRESSURE

The biggest hazard facing underwater tunnelers is the constant force of water pressure. The deeper the tunnel, the greater the force of the water pressure, which can sometimes crush the newly dug tunnel or force water into it through porous rock or soil. Because of the problems of water pressure, the first underwater tunnel, beneath London's Thames River, was not completed until 1843. This tunnel was made possible by the invention of a tunneling shield that protected the workers and supported the tunnel while it was being excavated and lined with brick.

Later underwater tunneling pioneers used compressed air in their tunnels to prevent water pressure from collapsing the digging site, but the use of compressed air carried with it severe health risks to workers. They often suffered from decompression sickness, which resulted in crippled joints or even death.

The Chunnel, while under the threat of the water pressure of the English Channel, could be constructed without the use of compressed air because of the innovative tunnel boring machines. These TBMs could support the freshly dug tunnel and line it immediately, greatly reducing the chance of a cave-in. Even with this sophisticated technology, however, the Chunnel did still suffer from unexpected water leakage and soggy conditions.

chines that were designed for dry tunneling. The British were forced to modify their machines as water poured in on their tunneling efforts in an early layer of unanticipated wet rock that persisted for nearly two miles. [It was] a potentially disastrous event . . . when the boring machines struck segments of rotten chalk, allowing water to roar into the tunnel. Since this stratum [layer] was too weak to support itself, tunnelers had to abandon the use of concrete lining for far stronger, but exorbitantly expensive, cast iron segments.[25]

The final solution was to build a stainless steel hood, thin enough to flex but strong enough to protect the workers and the concrete liner segments from falling rock. This way the TBM was able to continue through the bad ground and use the cheaper concrete liner. And because the tunnelers now knew where the other two tunnels would encounter the same bad ground, they prepared for it by injecting thin cement grout into the shattered rock layers ahead of those other tunnels to make their tunneling easier.

OTHER CHUNNEL OBSTACLES

There were also problems other than those encountered in the tunnel construction itself. In the fall of 1989, the Eurotunnel Group met with the financing banks in Paris and agreed to implement some cost reductions, since the project was now over budget and behind schedule. Shortly after, the Chunnel project passed the point of no return, where banks would have no choice but to continue funding the project, since to pull out at that time would result in a huge loss of money that they would never have the chance to regain in profits from a completed Chunnel.

In October 1989, the Eurotunnel Group was able to announce that about twenty-two miles of tunnel had been completed, nearly a quarter of the total, and the TBMs tunneling back into the land from the Sangatte and Shakespeare Cliff sites had nearly reached the sites for the two terminals.

There were human costs, however. There had been two deaths on the Chunnel project: a nineteen-year-old engineering assistant named Andrew McKenna had been crushed to death by a service train carrying spoil out of the tunnel. McKenna had

A MEDIA EVENT

The first breakthrough in the service tunnel was not only a celebration for those who were building the Chunnel, it was also planned as a media event, to be broadcast worldwide on television. Timing of the breakthrough was very important, since if it took place between 1:00 and 1:30 P.M. French time, then it would be broadcast on morning television in the United States and evening television in Japan. TML also wanted to use the video of the breakthrough in a longer, celebratory video that would be shown at the official celebration at Dover Castle that evening.

Because of all the media attention, many of the Chunnel's executives and managers wanted to be seen climbing through the connecting hole. It was also a dramatic episode to determine who would go through the opening first, after the two workers, Graham Fagg and Philippe Cozette, made the breakthrough. According to service tunnel manager David Denman as quoted in Drew Fetherston's book *The Chunnel,* "It was more of a problem figuring out who was going to go through to France than actually building the tunnel. There was a lot of people falling out with one another. I got fed up with it—They were arguing who was going to go through second, who was going to go through third." In all, several hundred people eventually stepped through the breakthrough into France and back again to celebrate the historic linking of the two countries on that December day.

apparently not heard the train approaching. His was the first death in the Chunnel. Another tunnel worker, David Simes, died when he was hit by a crane that transported tunnel segments on the TBM. He was walking in the crane operator's blind spot and could not be seen.

BREAKTHROUGH

Despite these obstacles, excitement was growing among the workers as the point where the two TBMs should meet was quickly approaching. Finally, on October 30, 1990, the atmosphere in the tunnel was tense. This would be the day that the two TBMs from England and France were supposed to meet in the middle of the Channel. It would be the true test of how well the guidance systems for the TBMs had functioned.

Only 330 feet lay between the two machines, and the British sent the drill probe ahead to drill a small hole. The French TBM Brigitte continued to bore through the rock until she met the tiny borehole from the British drill probe. If all the measurements and surveys were correct, Brigitte would run right into the drill hole, but if the calculations were off by even a little, it could be disastrous for the entire project.

The British team sent one of their engineers over to the French side to help as the moment of breakthrough drew closer. His name was Steve Cargo, and because all of his gear and

In 1991 French and British tunnel workers shake hands as they celebrate the perfect alignment of the two sides of the Chunnel.

equipment had "S. Cargo" on it, which sounded just like escargot, the French word for snail, he was known to his coworkers as the Snail. Cargo and the British team were linked by phone, and as the French TBM stopped where the drill hole should have been, theirs was a tense moment. Cargo reported that water was trickling through the rock face. Then Cargo said, "I've got it." The drill probe was pulled back, and the two countries were now linked by a very small passage, not even large enough for a man's hand. Cargo removed the end of the drill probe as a souvenir.

The linking of the two ends of the tunnel was officially celebrated on December 1, 1990. Two workers, one from each country, were chosen in a lottery to shake hands through the first

British Chunnel workers cheer the tunnel's completion in November 1990. The official Chunnel linking ceremony took place on December 1, 1990.

passage cut between the open tunnels. The two men chosen for the ceremony were good representatives of their respective countries. Philippe Cozette lived in a small village less than a mile from the French side of the tunnel, and he had no previous underground experience so he was trained while working on the Chunnel. He would eventually become a train engineer in the Chunnel system. Graham Fagg, the British worker, was typical of the British workforce because he was an experienced professional tunneler who had worked all over the world.

The historic moment is described by the British Broadcasting Corporation's Christopher Wain, reporting on December 1, 1990:

Construction workers have drilled through the final wall of rock to join the two halves of the Channel Tunnel and link Britain to France. The momentous breakthrough links the UK [Britain] to Europe for the first time since the Ice Age, 8,000 years ago. To a throng of cheers, construction workers celebrated with champagne—the only time alcohol has been allowed underground on the work site. French worker, Philippe Cozette, and his British counterpart, Graham Fagg, waved flags and shook hands as the first men able to walk between the two countries.[26]

The Chunnel project had made its first milestone, and there was now a passage under the English Channel.

5

THE FINAL DETAILS

Although the first breakthrough had been made, connecting France and England for the first time in history, the Chunnel project was far from over. The service tunnel was only the first of three tunnels that had to be dug beneath the Channel. There were also crossover caverns, piston relief ducts, and other areas necessary to running trains through the tunnel that had to be built. The running tunnels, which was the name given to the tunnels that would actually carry the train traffic, were also twenty-five feet in diameter, 50 percent larger than the service tunnel.

THE CATHEDRALS

Not only did the larger running tunnels have to be dug, but the large crossover caverns as well. There would be two of these crossover passages, about a third of the way in from each coast. These would accommodate the crossover links, sets of train tracks that would enable the Chunnel controllers to switch trains from one running tunnel to the other if one should have to be closed due to an accident or maintenance. This meant that the Chunnel would not have to be closed completely if one running tunnel was out of commission, since the trains could be switched over to the other track.

These crossover caverns were dubbed "cathedrals" by the workers because of their massive size; they were forty feet high and more than five hundred feet long. They would be the largest undersea caverns ever built.

Because the British had better geological conditions for their cathedral, with its location in a bed of firm, clay-rich chalk marl, they began to excavate the cavern by hand from the service tunnel. The two running tunnels would later intercept it. The French dug their cavern after the two running tunnels had already been excavated, actually removing the concrete tunnel lining rings that had just been installed by their TBM and then excavating a giant chamber over both tunnels.

Though the British had better rock conditions for creating their crossover chamber, they had difficulties with the lining of the cavern. Normally the space would be reinforced and strengthened with a layer of shotcrete, as well as twelve- to eighteen-foot-long steel dowels called rock bolts. These rock bolts were inserted through the shotcrete and into the walls,

Tunnelers work inside a crossover cavern, one of two passages designed to switch trains from one running tunnel to the other.

firmly attaching the concrete lining to the chalk. Four days after the British crossover cavern had been shotcreted, the roof started to sag and cracks appeared in the concrete. The steel reinforcing bars had buckled. The engineers finally discovered the cause of the problem: A pocket of water was resting on top of a layer of waterproof clay about thirteen feet above the cavern, and the weight of this water was pressing down on the cavern roof. According to Jack Lemley, an American construction engineer working on the project:

> A hydraulic head [water pocket] had built up over the chamber, and the water couldn't migrate through the rock. It started to add load to the crown [top] of the chamber. . . . We drilled several holes into it and drained it off, and the loads kind of stabilized. So it wasn't a long-term problem, but for three or four days we paid very careful attention.[27]

The uneasiness that the workers felt about the sagging ceiling was made worse by an account published in a local tabloid newspaper, in which a clairvoyant predicted that the tunnel would soon collapse and flood. The supervisors went back into the cavern first in order to convince the workers that it was safe to be there, despite the superstitions.

Workers also installed measuring devices deep in the chalk surrounding the caverns, allowing them to monitor the conditions of the ground. If they detected a problem or a weakness, they would increase the thickness of the concrete lining or add longer rock bolts.

The final lining of the caverns consisted of several layers. The first layer was the shotcrete, which was sprayed over a metal mesh. Next were two layers of fabric, one of which was plastic to keep water from seeping in. The final outer layer consisted of more shotcrete, which varied in thickness from twenty-three inches at the ceiling to more than three feet at floor level. More concrete was poured over the shotcrete to form the floor and end walls of the cavern. The floor was almost sixty feet wide, and at the very center the concrete was more than thirteen feet thick. The end walls, which would have to withstand the load of all the weight from the Channel above, were almost ten feet thick.

Finally, huge metal doors covered with a fireproof material were installed. They could be pulled closed to divide the

BRITAIN'S RABIES FEARS

One of the largest issues that tunnel proponents faced in winning over the British public to the idea of the Chunnel—and one that was extremely important in designing the two terminals and the entrances to the Chunnel—was that of rabies. Rabies is an infectious disease carried by dogs, cats, and other animals such as raccoons and squirrels. It can be transmitted to humans and is fatal without treatment. Britain had been free of rabies since 1902, when every dog suspected of having the disease was slaughtered. The British were extremely worried about the possibility of animals infected with rabies crossing to Britain through the Chunnel, infecting animals and reintroducing the disease in their country.

The Eurotunnel Group agreed to take serious measures to prevent rabid animals from entering the Chunnel. The first barrier was a fine mesh boundary fence that ran all around the terminals, extending below ground level to keep out burrowing animals. All vehicles within this fenced area were subject to checks and searches to make sure that no animals were smuggled in accidentally or intentionally.

During construction dog patrols and television surveillance helped prevent animals from entering the tunnels, and all entrances, pipes, ducts, and ventilation shafts were either covered with fine mesh wire or electrified to kill any intruding animals. Trash was not allowed to accumulate, as it might attract wild animals.

Passengers traveling to England are now allowed to bring their pets with them, but only after they have been examined by a vet and certified as being free of rabies. Otherwise, animals must be quarantined until they can be proven rabies-free. England still has not had a case of rabies since the Chunnel opened.

crossover cavern into two smaller caverns, closing one tunnel off from the other at that location. This would allow workers to close off one section of the tunnel from the other at the crossover cavern in case of fire and prevent the fire from spreading through the cavern to the other parts of the Chunnel.

The British caverns were eventually finished, despite the problems the builders encountered. As engineer Gordon Crighton said, the problems in the cavern were "bad but controllable. In any engineering job there are problems, if there were no problems, then ye wouldn't need engineers; they could put a bunch of bank clerks in there. . . . Making provisions for problems: that's what tunneling's all about."[28]

British workers install one of the massive fireproof metal doors designed to keep flames from spreading throughout the Chunnel in the event of fire.

PISTON RELIEF DUCTS

Another important component of the Chunnel also had to be dug by hand. These were the piston relief ducts, which were installed every 820 feet. They were vital to the safe operation of the trains. Because there was not enough room in the twenty-four-foot-diameter running tunnels for air to flow smoothly around the speeding trains, a locomotive would use too much energy simply pushing the air along. Tests showed that with piston relief ducts in place, the air in front of the train would be pushed into these ducts and into the other running tunnel. Behind the train, air would be sucked out of the ducts in the opposite direction. This would create a circular movement of air and limit the amount of energy needed by the locomotive just for air movement. The piston relief ducts would also have doors that could be closed in the event of fire, keeping smoke from spreading to other areas of the tunnels.

The piston relief ducts were all cut by hand with air spades, which are pneumatic jackhammers with a broad, chisel-shaped blade. It took strength and endurance for a worker to use an air spade, because it had to be lifted and held against the rock as it ate away at the rock face. The British tunnelers tended to use hand-tunneling techniques wherever possible, whereas the French often used roadheaders, which were small excavation machines.

MORE BREAKTHROUGHS

While the piston relief ducts were being dug, the two TBMs were still churning away toward each other to create the two running tunnels. And by the spring of 1991, the digging on the Chunnel project was coming to a close. On May 22, 1991, the two TBMs met in the middle of the northern running tunnel, which would carry passengers from England to France. A month later, on June 28, the French TBM finished the last few yards of digging and met the British in the southern tunnel. After four years of digging, the last tunnel had been completed. The three tunnels dug beneath the English Channel, along with nine smaller entrance tunnels that funneled trains into and out of the two terminals and the tunnel entrances, added up to over ninety miles of tunnel, and the amount of spoil removed from them could cover sixty-eight football fields.

The British TBMs had been driven down into the Channel bed and gutted of their machinery and useful components. Then the shells were pumped full of concrete and covered over, to remain there forever. Then the French TBMs simply drove over the entombed British TBMs and out through the completed portion of the tunnel.

The land tunnels were also nearing completion. They had received less attention in the press, but were often just as difficult to construct as the underwater tunnels. In the Holywell Coombe section of tunnel between Shakespeare Cliff and the Folkestone terminal, the tunnel was created by a method called cut and cover, where the tunnel's path was excavated and lined with a long concrete box. This was then covered over with earth. The tunnel section under Castle Hill was built using shotcrete to form the tunnel structure.

With all of the tunneling completed, the engineers and workers on the Chunnel still had a great deal of work to do, but the most dangerous and unpredictable aspect had been completed. It was time to fine-tune the details and install the equipment to make the Chunnel into a true link.

TRAIN TRACKS

First, the tunnels needed to be equipped for the rail traffic they would soon carry. Previously, both ends of the tunnels had little construction railways necessary for transporting men and materials to and from the work sites. When the two ends of the construction railway in the service tunnel were joined, the first train to actually travel from England to France was one of these work trains. Soon after, the construction railway's tracks were removed so that permanent track could be installed. The service tunnel was given a concrete roadbed to accommodate the rubber-tired service vehicles that would eventually be used there: two tractors on either ends of a passenger pod equipped with seats, since there would not be enough room to turn around in the service tunnel.

The final train tracks in the running tunnels consisted of rails that did not rest on wooden ties placed across the rail bed, like most railroads, but rather on rows of short concrete blocks. These blocks were encased in rubber shoes that absorbed shock and noise. The rails themselves, in six-hundred-foot sections with three hundred concrete blocks already attached, were set on the surface of a first layer of concrete that was poured on the tunnel floors. Once the rails were in place a work train returned

EYEWITNESS TO A BREAKTHROUGH

The British and French TBMs broke through the south-running tunnel, the last tunnel to be completed, on June 28, 1991. Cathy Newman, a reporter for *National Geographic* magazine, was an eyewitness to the event as described in her article "The Light at the End of the Chunnel":

> Looking up, I imagine 180 feet of Channel above my head—ferries, tankers, a Dover sole [fish] or two . . . the grating of the TBM interrupts my reverie. Its cutterhead—a huge wheel with tungsten-tipped teeth—chews into the last trace of rock separating England from France. Music blares, and lights glare. Several Frenchmen scramble through. . . . Strangely moving, this connecting of countries. Champagne corks pop, and French workers hug British counterparts. "I might have opposed it 30 years ago, but now it's my tunnel," an Englishman says. French tunnelers are still climbing through. "So many," I say, turning to a French official. "And there are 56 million more behind them," he replies.

and poured another layer of concrete on top to embed the concrete blocks.

Trackside signals were also installed to signal the Eurotunnel trains when to stop and go and to manage the traffic in the tunnel. On each end of the Chunnel the shuttle trains would have to be switched off the single tunnel track onto one of three loop tracks that brought trains around to the platform area, and then onto one of ten platform tracks where passengers would get on and off. Trains had to be slowed and stopped automatically, and the controllers in the terminals had to know where every train was at every moment, inside the terminals and the running tunnels.

The tracks and signal systems were complex enough, but the actual trains that had been ordered for the Eurotunnel system would be one of the biggest issues that beset the completion and successful opening of the Chunnel.

A Euroshuttle train bound for London leaves a station in Paris. The locomotives of the Chunnel train were the most powerful ever designed.

ROLLING STOCK

The traffic anticipated for the Chunnel required several different types of rolling stock, or the railroad shuttles and wagons needed to carry passengers and vehicles. Passengers would be able to travel in traditional coaches with seats if they did not wish to transport their vehicles, or they could use the passenger shuttles. The traditional passenger coaches made up the Eurostar trains, each with room for 766 passengers in eighteen rail cars. These trains were capable of traveling at speeds as high as one hundred miles per hour.

A passenger shuttle train was made up of three different types of rail cars: loading wagons, which were the "ramp" cars that vehicles would use to actually drive onto the train, and single- and double-decker vehicle carriers. Heavier wagons were also constructed specifically to carry large trucks. Cars and trucks could be driven onto these vehicle carriers and their drivers could either remain in the vehicles or walk around in the shuttle car. These different types of rail cars would be linked together and have a locomotive at each end of the train. This enabled the train to head back to the other end of the Chunnel without having to turn around.

The passenger shuttles were the largest railroad wagons ever built, each eighty-five feet long and able to carry approximately twenty-six tons of vehicles. Because they were so large, they were only able to operate in the Chunnel environment with its controlled conditions. Above ground, the strong winds off the Channel would easily derail them.

Pictured are some of the Euroshuttle's first passengers, traveling alongside their vehicles parked in one of the train's enormous passenger cars.

The Chunnel locomotives were the most powerful locomotives in the world. Not only did they have to push or pull a loaded train, but if one of the locomotives broke down, then the other would have to be able to start up and push the train. If both locomotives failed, then the next train that came along would have to have enough power to push the stalled train to the station, as well as its own train. These locomotives were powered by electricity, running through overhead cables in the tunnels. A total of thirty-eight locomotives were constructed: enough for seventeen complete trains plus four spares.

The Eurotunnel Group decided that the shuttles would be equipped with a steel roll-up door on each end, with a pass-through door on either side for passengers to use if they needed to exit the car while the train was underway. These pass doors were to be six hundred millimeters [slightly over twenty-three inches] wide even though the same type of doors in buildings were usually seven hundred millimeters [approximately twenty-seven inches] wide. Eurotunnel initially ordered 252 shuttles with this size pass door, but the intergovernmental commission and the safety committee, which were overseeing safety in the Chunnel, ultimately required the larger-size pass door. This added a cost of almost $107 million to the project, and added ten months to the delivery schedule.

SAFETY SYSTEMS

Safety precautions were one of the major issues that the engineers designing the Chunnel had to contend with. There were many different scenarios that could result in disaster inside the Chunnel: fire, natural disasters such as earthquakes, and terrorism. The Chunnel ended up being an extraordinarily safe tunnel, because it combined the safety philosophies of both the English and the French: The French preferred a hands-on approach, and the English utilized computers that could anticipate and automatically deal with safety hazards.

Special evacuation teams practiced fire drills and bomb threat evacuations before the Chunnel even opened. The passenger shuttle cars and the carrier wagons for vehicles were manufactured with fire safety in mind, with features such as fire safety curtains that could prevent flames from spreading from one area to another and doorways wide enough to evacuate the cars quickly.

It was also discovered that the trains, once they had been tested, produced an unexpected amount of heat. The temperatures around the test tracks rose to as high as 140°F, which made the tunnels dangerously hot. The solution was to pump cold water through a pipeline created within the tunnels and caverns. The cold water would absorb heat and then be pumped to cooling stations on both ends of the Chunnel, where it would be chilled again and recirculated.

DRIVING A CHUNNEL LOCOMOTIVE

The Chunnel's locomotives are the most powerful in the world, hauling trains over two thousand tons in weight at speeds of up to one hundred miles per hour. Driving one of these trains is an enormous responsibility for the engineer.

The locomotive driver sits at an instrument panel called the driver's console. On the right side of the console is a power controller that can be set to either forward or reverse the train. The engineer moves it forward to make the train move faster in either direction, while pulling back on the power controller applies enough brake to keep the train from gaining too much speed when going downhill. The main brake lever is on the left side of the console, and it not only slows the locomotive but is connected to the brakes on the entire train, including the shuttle cars. At the far left is a separate braking lever that uses only the locomotive's air brakes, and this is used when the locomotive is being driven on its own, without an attached train. The engineer can control the train in either a sitting or standing position.

There are no side windows in the Chunnel locomotives, because engineers can be affected by "segment flicker," a condition caused by a series of similar objects such as lights rushing by the windows. This can make a driver sleepy.

The driver is in constant communication with the Rail Control Center in Folkestone and also receives continuous feedback from different sensors within the train and the tunnel itself. There is also a train captain, who sits in the other locomotive at the rear of the train and can drive the train if something goes wrong with the front locomotive.

The shuttle cars had to be constructed to withstand fire, which was one of the biggest safety fears in the Chunnel. Once the shuttle had a full load of vehicles, the end of each shuttle car had to be closed in case fire broke out in one of the vehicles on-board. According to the rules set forth by the Chunnel's planners:

> The Heavy Goods Vehicle shuttle trains are made up of two rakes of wagons [and] one Amenity coach for the . . . [truck] drivers, with a locomotive at either end of the train. A rake comprises 14 or 15 carrier wagons with a loader wagon at each end. One end of each loader wagon contains two on-board fire detection units . . . with a [breathing] tube and a smoke detector. Information on the condition of this system is transmitted directly to the . . . drivers' cabin. The materials used in the construction of the Amenity Coach [which serves food and drink to the truck drivers] meet strict fire resistance, smoke emission, toxicity and flammability requirements. The ends of the Amenity Coach have a 30 minute fire resistance. The access doors are equipped with inflatable seals.[29]

A TERMINAL AT EACH END

With the Chunnel equipment ordered, the only other major construction left to finish were the two terminals in Folkestone and Coquelles. The two terminals at either end of the Chunnel needed to be completed for the opening of the tunnel to train traffic. England's Folkestone terminal, the rail control center for the entire Chunnel, is where controllers would sit in front of a huge electronic diagram of the entire Chunnel and monitor temperature, air, and traffic conditions. The Coquelles terminal in France had an identical control system that could take over operations from Folkestone in the event of an emergency. Both terminals were also responsible for monitoring the rail traffic in and out of their own area.

The Folkestone terminal had to meet stringent environmental restrictions to minimize the impact of the terminal area on the surrounding landscape. The terminal buildings were limited to thirteen feet in height, visual and acoustic screening had to be provided to protect residents in nearby villages, and water and air quality were monitored throughout the construction process. Three buildings that were listed as being historically

This 1992 photo shows sections of the Chunnel's main terminal on the English side in Folkestone under construction.

important were dismantled and catalogued so that they could be rebuilt elsewhere. Because the terminal area included the site of an ancient woodland, a new woodland area had to be created outside the terminal with the soil and seedlings collected from the original site.

Construction on the Folkestone terminal began in 1988 with a major landfill project necessary for creating the level area needed for the railway system. The buildings constructed at the terminal include a control tower, border control buildings for the French and British authorities, passenger and freight buildings, security, and headquarters for the operations staff. Smaller structures also had to be built, including bridges over the tracks, access ramps, and platforms for passengers and vehicles to board the trains.

The Coquelles terminal in France also required millions of cubic feet of dirt fill to be spread, compressed, and leveled for the terminal site. Because the land was low and swampy, there had to be drainage of excess water. The contractors also had to be sure to maintain the wetland habitat areas for any wildlife in the area. The French terminal covers an area as large as an airport, almost two thousand acres. The buildings there include the Eurotunnel head office, an additional control tower, passenger terminals, freight terminals, and border control areas. The Coquelles terminal also includes a viaduct bridge for passenger cars that crosses several lake areas.

By the end of 1993 the construction of the two terminals was nearing completion. Track, electrical and ventilation systems, as well as signaling, were also close to being completely installed. The Chunnel could now begin testing in preparation for its grand opening.

6

THE CHUNNEL OPENS

The long-held dream of linking Britain and France was about to become a reality, ushering in a new era for both countries. After more than six years of construction, multiple problems with equipment, TBMs, and water, and a final price tag of $16 billion (and some said that the true cost was nearer to $21 billion), the Chunnel was ready to be opened.

A TEST RUN

On December 10, 1993, the Eurotunnel Group planned its first test run through the entire Chunnel. Two trains, one in Paris and one at Victoria Station in London, would carry their passengers through the Chunnel to the other side, with the Paris train making a round-trip back to France for the official festivities. A ceremony at the Coquelles terminal would include the official handing over of the tunnel from the contractors to the Eurotunnel Group. This was supposed to signify that all work on the Chunnel was completed.

Four hundred invitations were sent out to the people who had worked on the Eurotunnel as well as dignitaries and top business people. There were some last-minute problems, however: The British government would not allow the new, high-speed Eurostar trains to make the trip because they had not yet been tested to meet safety requirements. The guests would have to ride in an ordinary first-class passenger train to Folkestone and then switch to another train for the journey through the tunnel, since ordinary first-class trains did not run on the same kind of overhead power as the Chunnel trains did. The substitute train was also narrower than the Chunnel trains, and the passengers had to use a temporary bridge to board the train at the Folkestone station.

The French train made the first round-trip through the Chunnel, followed two hours later by the British train, which left the Folkestone terminal at 6 P.M. As a safety precaution, the controllers allowed only one train in the Chunnel at a time. Finally

A worker installs signs demarcating the Anglo-French border in the Chunnel, which officially opened for business on May 6, 1994.

the British train passed through the Chunnel in twenty-two minutes, arriving at the Coquelles terminal to the music of "It's a Long Way to Tipperary," a famous Irish World War I marching song. The two trainloads of passengers met under a huge tent for champagne, food, music, and fireworks. The Chunnel had been successfully completed at last.

A GRAND OPENING

Although the first trains had passed beneath the Channel, the Chunnel was not yet open for business. There were still small details to be completed before the Chunnel would be open to the public, such as additional emergency drills and safety testing. Finally, six months later on May 6, 1994, Queen Elizabeth of England and President François Mitterrand of France marked the official opening of the Chunnel. The queen boarded a Eurostar luxury train in London and made the trip through the Chunnel to Coquelles, where she was met by President Mitterrand. Together they cut a huge ribbon at the Coquelles terminal and praised the efforts of all the workers who had built the Chunnel. President Mitterrand called the Chunnel "a major asset for the strengthening of the European Union, a decisive element in the elaboration of the Common Market, [and] another step toward the coming together of peoples."[30] Queen Elizabeth hailed the tunnel as "a successful combination of French élan [style] and British pragmatism."[31]

The two world leaders then climbed into the queen's car and drove onto the vehicle shuttle for the trip back to England. The ceremonies ended with a celebratory banquet inside the British crossover cavern of the Chunnel.

TRAVELING THROUGH THE CHUNNEL

Traveling through the Chunnel has become increasingly popular since it opened for business in 1994. Travelers can drive their own cars to the terminals in France or England and make their way through a series of tollbooths and ramps. They then drive directly onto one of Eurotunnel's Le Shuttle trains, which can carry over two hundred automobiles per train. Once on the shuttle, drivers can either stay inside their vehicles or walk around inside the shuttle car, which have restrooms. The trip takes about thirty minutes, plus another thirty minutes for loading and unloading. Truck drivers load their trucks onto special vehicle transporters and then spend the travel time in a special club car at the front of the train, where they can eat and stretch their legs. Trucks are not allowed to carry hazardous cargo such as toxic or explosive substances inside the Chunnel.

Passengers without cars can travel on the high-speed Eurostar trains that run between London and Paris with roughly three hours of travel time. These trains are regular passenger trains with coach seating and dining cars.

By the summer of 1994 the Chunnel was open for regular passenger traffic. The company's goal was to have one-third of the 18.5 million travelers who annually crossed the English Channel by boat or airplane use the new Chunnel by 1995. In March 1995, when the Eurotunnel Group's advertising invited travelers to come to the Folkestone terminal and cross through the Chunnel, so many travelers showed up that the terminal was overwhelmed and the police had to be called to deal with the traffic.

By the fall of 1996 between 70 and 80 percent of all passengers between England and France were using the Chunnel, and half of the automobiles between Dover and Calais were using the Chunnel's shuttles. The Eurotunnel Group still owed billions

French president François Mitterrand and British queen Elizabeth II participate in the ribbon cutting ceremony at the Chunnel's Coquelles terminal.

of dollars to its investors, but it was beginning to earn profits from its customers. Unfortunately, the Chunnel was also about to experience its first real emergency.

FIRE IN THE CHUNNEL

On the evening of November 18, 1996, a train left the Coquelles terminal at 9:42 P.M. and headed toward Folkestone. It was carrying twenty-nine trucks in open-sided vehicle carriers. The drivers of these trucks had moved to the club car at the front of the shuttle, and some were already eating dinner. As the train moved into the south-running tunnel, four witnesses reported seeing a fire under one of the trucks on the vehicle carrier. The witnesses said that the fire was a good size, with flames roughly six feet high.

The witnesses, including two security patrolmen, notified the Rail Control Center at Folkestone. The engineer of the train also received a fire alarm from his rear locomotive, which did not routinely have a driver. The tunnel's fire-detection system also began to notify the control center of fire in the tunnel. The controllers stopped other trains from entering the tunnel and closed the piston relief ducts to keep smoke from spreading to the other tunnel.

The driver followed the established procedure of continuing toward the other end of the tunnel, but then he received an alarm that one of the propping jacks on a shuttle car, which were used much like a kickstand on a bicycle to stabilize the car during loading and unloading, might be in the down position. Because this could derail the train, the engineer had to stop the train. When he did, a wave of smoke washed forward over the train and seeped into the club car behind the locomotive where thirty-one passengers (one of whom was a pregnant woman) were sitting. The train was now eleven miles from the French portal and nineteen miles from the British end of the tunnel. The smoke outside was so thick that the engineer could not read the marker on the wall to tell the controllers exactly what section of tunnel he was in. From their sensor information the controllers only knew that the train was in a certain area of the track.

Unfortunately, once the train stopped, an employee in the club car opened the exterior door, and smoke billowed into the car. Some of the passengers panicked and wanted to exit the car, but the train steward prevented this since conditions outside

ILLEGAL IMMIGRANTS

The opening of the Chunnel has had unexpected conse-
quences that planners had not prepared for. One of the
largest problems that the Chunnel must deal with on a daily
basis is that of immigrants who try to cross from France into
England illegally. Many of these people are from Afghan-
istan, Iran, Russia, and the Czech Republic, and they are
seeking a better life in England, where the immigration laws
are more relaxed than in the rest of Europe. These refugees
gather in Sangatte because it is the closest town to the Chunnel, and their numbers are so great that the Red Cross eventually built a shelter for them in a giant warehouse left from
the Chunnel's construction. Often the shelter, which was designed for five hundred, holds more than a thousand
refugees a night, people who would otherwise be sleeping
on the streets of Sangatte.

The refugees gather every night and attempt to jump
onto the shuttle trains without being seen. Others hide on
bridge overpasses and try to jump onto trucks that will be
loaded in the shuttle. These attempts to cross through the
tunnel can be very dangerous, as refugees have been found
suffocated in sealed trucks, nearly frozen to death beneath
trains, or killed after getting stuck between the trains and
the train platform.

Those who are caught are merely released back into
Sangatte and try again another night. The Eurotunnel must
pay a fine to the British government for every refugee who
successfully stows away and makes it to Britain. Because of
this, the company has put many barriers in place, such as
over a hundred security guards, cameras at every area of the

the car were worse than those inside. Instead, the passengers
were told to lie on the floor and cover their faces with wet nap-
kins. After twenty minutes, French firefighters arrived and evac-
uated all the passengers and crew through the service tunnel.
Two of them, a driver and the pregnant woman, were more seriously injured than the others and had to be taken by helicopter
to a hospital, but all the victims who suffered from smoke in-
halation did recover.

Meanwhile, the fire itself grew worse. One of the trucks
loaded on the vehicle carrier was carrying twenty tons of frozen

terminal, barbed wire and electric fencing, and dogs. All this has cost Eurotunnel more than $4 million, but refugees still make it through. In December 2001 over five hundred refugees rushed the terminal at Sangatte, breaking down fences, and were finally stopped by French police using tear gas. Eurotunnel says that in the first half of the year 2001 alone, roughly 18,500 immigrants tried to cross through the Chunnel.

A French security officer arrests a man trying to enter Britain illegally by hiding in a truck near the Chunnel entrance.

fat, and when it caught fire it caused an explosion that sent shock waves through the tunnel. Firefighters had to deal with extreme heat and other hazards, according to Ed Comeau and Alisa Wolf in their article "Fire in the Chunnel!":

> Firefighters also had to dodge pieces of concrete falling from the tunnel ceilings and walls. They were advised not to look up in order to avoid injuries. This falling debris collected on the shuttle roofs, which ultimately collapsed into V shapes. The debris also collected on the

In November 1996 officials survey the damage caused to a section of the Chunnel after a fire that started on a train spread to the tunnel.

tunnel walkways, creating a sloping surface that was difficult to walk on. It, too, was intensely hot, according to firefighters whose soles were burned from standing on them.[32]

The fire was finally extinguished by 5:00 A.M. the next morning, but the damage to the tunnel was considerable. The heat of the fire, estimated to have reached over 2,000°F, dislodged the concrete liner of the tunnel and exposed some of the fiberglass insulation. The thickness of the liner was reduced from fifteen inches to as little as six inches, and where the fire was most intense, the lining was now less than an inch thick. All of the steel reinforcing in the concrete was exposed. Over sixteen hundred feet of track were destroyed, as well as the power supply for the locomotives and the track circuits in the area of the fire. Besides the damage to the tunnel, fifteen vehicle carriers and the locomotive were damaged, and ten shuttle passenger cars were destroyed.

NEW SAFETY PROCEDURES

As a result of the fire, the Chunnel was closed completely for fifteen days. The Eurotunnel Group faced criticism for the way the fire was handled and the efficiency of the safety systems and procedures used in the tunnels. Many people blamed the fire on the open-sided vehicle carriers used in the Chunnel, which allowed the fire to spread from one truck to the entire train. Britain's Consumers' Association stated its concerns about the safety of the Chunnel, including the evacuation procedures and the fact that passengers rode in enclosed tourist shuttles along with their cars and the combustible fuel within those cars.

In May 1997 the Channel Tunnel Safety Authority issued an official report on the fire and made thirty-six safety recommendations. The report also concluded that insufficient staff training

TERRORISM

The Chunnel has always been considered as less vulnerable to acts of terrorism than a bridge would have been, but terrorism has been a fact of life in Europe and England long before September 11, 2001, when Americans became more aware of the potential for acts of terrorism in everyday life. The Irish Republican Army, or IRA, a group that uses terrorism to protest the British rule of Ireland, plotted in 1996 to blow up part of the Chunnel. British police found out about the attacks and were able to stop them, arresting five terrorists and killing another. The police discovered a large cache of explosives, weapons, and ammunition that was to be used to destroy the Chunnel. Since this incident, no other serious terrorist threats have been made against the Chunnel.

Eurotunnel has taken precautions, however. The United States has developed a new high-tech sensor device called the EGIS, which can detect minute amounts of the residue used to make explosives. The Eurotunnel service uses this sensor to screen cars boarding the Chunnel shuttles. Extra security such as guard patrols, surveillance cameras, and electric fencing are already in place due to the surging numbers of illegal immigrants, who could also be terrorist threats, trying to stow away into Britain.

had led to delays and mistakes in dealing with the fire. Eurotunnel later said that most of the recommendations had been put into place. According to a spokeswoman for Eurotunnel, "We have learnt lessons from the fire and the main lessons were that our procedures and training could be improved and that some of our procedures were too complex."[33]

A marvel of modern engineering, the Chunnel attracts millions of passengers every year, linking Britain more closely to Europe than at any other point in history.

It took 140 workers over six months to repair the damage to the Chunnel, at a cost of over $80 million. While repairs were underway, the Chunnel continued to operate. Since the north tunnel was not damaged, trains simply crossed over to the north tunnel to avoid the damaged section of the south tunnel. A survey taken soon after the fire found that most of the Chunnel's passengers still thought that the Chunnel was safe.

THE FUTURE OF THE CHUNNEL

The Chunnel continues to attract more and more passengers, and in its first six years of operation almost 60 million people have passed through its tunnels. Eurotunnel still has a huge debt from the Chunnel's construction, which it is hoping to pay off by 2028. Eurotunnel has also established a group to study proposals for another tunnel to be constructed by 2012, a tunnel that would allow motorists to drive their own vehicles beneath the Channel. This would give travelers the full range of options for crossing the Channel, either by ferry, train tunnel, or automotive tunnel.

Despite the huge obstacles involved in planning, financing, and construction, the Chunnel successfully fulfilled its mission to link the two countries with a fast, safe, and efficient rail service. It permanently linked two countries that once viewed each other with distrust, and it also brought England into the European marketplace. As Eurotunnel's French chairman André Bénard said in an article in *National Geographic* magazine, "The tunnel crystallizes a moment in history. We've brought Britain closer to Europe. There's no turning back."[34]

NOTES

Introduction: Linking Two Countries
1. William Shakespeare, *Richard II*, act 2, scene 1. New York: New American Library, 1963, pp. 66–67.

Chapter 1: A Channel History
2. Drew Fetherston, *The Chunnel: The Amazing Story of the Undersea Crossing of the English Channel*. New York: Random House, 1997, pp. 30–31.
3. Quoted in Fetherston, *The Chunnel*, p. 32.
4. Fetherston, *The Chunnel*, pp. 37–38.
5. Quoted in Thomas Whiteside, *The Tunnel Under the Channel*. New York: Simon and Schuster, 1962, p. 22.
6. Quoted in Whiteside, *The Tunnel Under the Channel*, p. 36.
7. Quoted in Fetherston, *The Chunnel*, p. 40.
8. Quoted in Whiteside, *The Tunnel Under the Channel*, p. 45.
9. Quoted in Fetherston, *The Chunnel*, pp. 87–88.
10. Quoted in Fetherston, *The Chunnel*, p. 88.
11. Quoted in Fetherston, *The Chunnel*, p. 96.

Chapter 2: A Winning Design
12. John Neerhout Jr., "The Making of the Channel Tunnel: A Modern Day Wonder." Gould Distinguished Lecture Series, University of Utah, 1995, p. 4.
13. Quoted in Neerhout, "The Making of the Channel Tunnel," p. 4.
14. Fetherston, *The Chunnel*, p. 96.
15. *Facts On File World News Digest*, "Other International News: U.K., France OK Channel Rail Link," January 24, 1986, p. 1. www.2facts.com/TempFiles/1986001230.htm.
16. Quoted in Fetherston, *The Chunnel*, p. 7.
17. Fetherston, *The Chunnel*, p. 130.

Chapter 3: Preparing to Tunnel
18. David Macaulay, *Building Big*. Boston: Houghton Mifflin, 2000, p. 81.
19. Fetherston, *The Chunnel*, p. 185.
20. Neerhout, "The Making of the Channel Tunnel," p. 8.
21. Fetherston, *The Chunnel*, p. 18.

Chapter 4: Tunneling

22. David Macaulay, *Building Big*, p. 79.

23. Quoted in Fetherston, *The Chunnel*, p. 22.

24. Fetherston, *The Chunnel*, p. 224.

25. Stephen Johnson and Roberto T. Leon, *Encyclopedia of Bridges and Tunnels*. New York: Checkmark Books, 2002, p. 112.

26. Christopher Wain, "On This Day: 1 December, 1990," British Broadcasting Corporation, p. 1. http://news.bbc.co.uk/onthis day/low/dates/stories/december/1/newsid_2516000/2516473. stm.

Chapter 5: The Final Details

27. Quoted in Fetherston, *The Chunnel*, p. 337.

28. Quoted in Fetherston, *The Chunnel*, p. 339.

29. United Kingdom Department for Transport, European and International Railways, "Inquiry into the Fire on Heavy Goods Vehicle Shuttle," November 18, 1996. www.dft.gov. uk/stellent/groups/dft_railways/documents/page/dft_rail ways_504363-03.hcsp#P276_23198.

Chapter 6: The Chunnel Opens

30. Quoted in *Facts On File World News Digest*, "Channel Tunnel Inaugurated: Fall Opening for Customers Seen," May 26, 1994, p. 2. www.2facts.com/TempFiles/1994057224.htm.

31. Quoted in *Facts On File World News Digest*, "Channel Tunnel Inaugurated," p. 2.

32. Ed Comeau and Alisa Wolf, "Fire in the Chunnel!" *National Fire Protection Association Journal*, March/April 1997, p. 5.

33. Quoted in British Broadcasting Corporation, "Chunnel Trains 'Safer Than Ever'—Eurotunnel," November 18, 1997. http://news.bbc.co.uk/1/hi/uk/32467.stm.

34. Quoted in Cathy Newman, "The Light at the End of the Chunnel," *National Geographic*, May 1994, p. 47.

FOR FURTHER READING

Books

Lionel Bender, *Engineers at Work Series: Eurotunnel.* New York: Scholastic, 1990. A look at the building of the Chunnel while it was still under construction.

Sandy Donovan, *The Channel Tunnel.* Minneapolis, MN: Lerner, 2003. A recent look at the Chunnel's construction, including current problems with immigration.

Jil Fine, *The Chunnel: The Building of a 200-Year-Old Dream.* Danbury, CT: Childrens, 2004. A high-interest/low-reading-level book on the Chunnel's construction.

Joanne Mattern, *The Chunnel.* Farmington Hills, MI: Blackbirch, 2004. A look at the Chunnel's construction for younger readers.

Web Sites

Building Big (www.pbs.org/wgbh/buildingbig). The home page for the PBS series *Building Big*, with information and activities about tunnels and the Chunnel.

Cool Stuff and Incredible Feats of Construction (www.construct myfuture.com/stu-coolstuff.html). Includes information about the Channel tunnel's construction in its "Top Ten Construction Feats of the 20th Century."

Eurotunnel (www.eurotunnel.com). The official site for Eurotunnel, which operates the Chunnel. Includes a history, interesting facts, and travel information.

World's Longest Tunnel Page (http://home.no.net/lotsberg/index.html). All about the world's longest tunnels, including the Chunnel, organized by country and type. Also includes tunneling history and excellent links.

Works Consulted

Books

Nigel Calder, *The English Channel.* New York: Penguin, 1987. A tour of the English Channel with a chapter devoted to plans for a Channel tunnel.

Drew Fetherston, *The Chunnel: The Amazing Story of the Undersea Crossing of the English Channel.* New York: Random House, 1997. The most complete book available on the construction of the Channel tunnel.

Stephen Johnson and Roberto T. Leon, *Encyclopedia of Bridges and Tunnels.* New York: Checkmark Books, 2002. An overview of bridge and tunnel construction throughout the world, with examples of specific structures.

David Macaulay, *Building Big.* Boston: Houghton Mifflin, 2000. An excellent book on different kinds of construction, with a section on tunneling and the Chunnel.

William Shakespeare, *Richard II.* New York: New American Library, 1963. One of Shakespeare's plays that contains a quote about England and the protection provided by the Channel.

Thomas Whiteside, *The Tunnel Under the Channel.* New York: Simon and Schuster, 1962. Although this book predates the Chunnel's construction, it gives an excellent history of other earlier attempts to build a Channel link.

Periodicals

Ed Comeau and Alisa Wolf, "Fire in the Chunnel!" *National Fire Protection Association Journal*, March/April 1997.

Cathy Newman, "The Light at the End of the Chunnel," *National Geographic*, May 1994.

Internet Sources

British Broadcasting Corporation, "Chunnel Row over Refugee Camp," August 21, 2004. http://news.bbc.co.uk/1/hi/world/europe/1502161.stm.

———, "Chunnel Trains 'Safer Than Ever'—Eurotunnel," November 18, 1997. http://news.bbc.co.uk/1/hi/uk/32467.stm.

Engineering.Com, "The Chunnel," July 11, 2004. www.engineering.com/content/ContentDisplay?contendid=41007026.

Eurotunnel, "About Us: Traffic Figures," 2004. www.eurotunnel.com/ukMain/ukcCompany/ukcAboutUs/ukpAboutUsTraffic.

Facts On File World News Digest, "Channel Tunnel Inaugurated: Fall Opening for Customers Seen," May 26, 1994. www.2facts.com/TempFiles/1994057224.htm.

———, "U.K., France OK Channel Rail Link", January 24, 1986. www.2facts.com/TempFiles/1986001230.htm.

John Neerhout Jr., "The Making of the Channel Tunnel: A Modern Day Wonder," Gould Distinguished Lecture Series, University of Utah, October 5, 1995. www.lib.utah.edu/gould/lecture95.html.

United Kingdom Department for Transport, European and International Railways, "Inquiry into the Fire on Heavy Goods Vehicle Shuttle," November 18, 1996. www.dft.gov.uk/stellent/groups/dft_railways/documents/page/dft_railways_504363-03.hcsp#P276_23198.

USA Today, "Refugees Rush 'Chunnel,'" Associated Press, December 26, 2001. www.usatoday.com/news/world/2001/12/26/chunnel.htm.

Christopher Wain, "On This Day: 1 December 1990," British Broadcasting Corporation, December 1, 1990. http://news.bbc.co.uk/onthisday/low/dates/stories/december/1/newsid_2516000/2516473.stm.

INDEX

106

Picture Credits

ABOUT THE AUTHOR

Marcia Amidon Lüsted has a degree in English and secondary education and has worked as a middle school English teacher, bookseller, and musician. She lives in Hancock, New Hampshire, with her husband and three sons.